NO FLOWERS . . . JUST LOTS OF JOY

No Flowers ...
just lots of joy

FIONA CASTLE
with Jan Greenough

KINGSWAY PUBLICATIONS
EASTBOURNE

First published 1996
Reprinted 1996, 1997

Unless otherwise indicated, biblical quotations are from the
New International Version © 1973, 1978, 1982 by the
International Bible Society

ISBN 0 85476 624 3

Front cover photo: Paul Yates

Designed and produced by
Bookprint Creative Services
P.O. Box 827, BN21, 3YJ, England for
KINGSWAY PUBLICATIONS LTD
Lottsbridge Drove, Eastboure, E. Sussex BN23 6NT.
Printed in Great Britain.

Contents

Foreword

This is a book for everyone. Having started to read it I could not put it down although I should have been doing other things. It is an unvarnished record of an ordinary woman confronting dying, death and bereavement in extraordinary circumstances. I was an observer of some of the events recorded in the book and so I know that this is real stuff that is being handled. In a real sense it is not so much about death and dying as it is about life and living.

Roy Castle was a straightforward, down-to-earth, realistic, no-nonsense, shunning humbug Yorkshire man with a warm and generous heart. He was my friend for twenty years, and in the earliest days I quickly realised that with Roy what you saw was what you got. I expected and looked for a 'public image'—there was none! Over a life-time of relating to people I have discovered that this is a rare characteristic. He was incredibly talented yet unself-conscious. Frank Bruno, the former World Heavyweight Boxing Champion, said of him, 'He could relate to dustbin men and royalty. He was a nice somebody in showbusiness. I remember him like a diamond.'

Fiona confronts life in a similarly unpretentious way—there are situations to be dealt with; circumstances to be handled; needs to be met; people to be cared for; lives to be loved; issues to be resolved; faith to be expressed; and a God to be trusted. This is theology with shoes on. This is preaching—and only with words where necessary. This is Christianity with a heart and reality.

'When I die I shall rot, and nothing of my ego shall survive. . . . There is darkness without and when I die there will be darkness within. There is no splendour, no vastness anywhere; only triviality for a moment, and then nothing.' So Betrand Russell expresses the ultimate horror of atheism.

Tom Stoppard in *Rosencrantz and Guildenstern Are Dead* expresses the same despair in a terrifying way:

Death is not anything . . . death is not . . .
It's the absence of presence, nothing more . . .
The endless time of never coming back
A gap you can't see, and when the wind blows through it
  it makes no sound.

'Not so!' cries Jesus. 'I am the one who raises the dead and gives them life again. Anyone who believes in me, even though he dies like anyone else, shall live again. He is given eternal life for believing in me and shall never perish.'

It was with this confidence Roy died. It is with this confidence Fiona lives and shares her life. This reality alone enables her to face life with gallantry, and death without fear. Of course there are tears and poignant moments and unanswered questions and loneliness and a deep sense of loss, but God is able to give resources to handle these realities (really, really able!).

I wish this book had been written when I faced my own 'valley of the shadow', or at least when I started out in ministry, for it deals with issues that are deeply personal, very difficult to define and even more difficult to deal with. Having read it you will be profoundly grateful for those who have personally influenced and enriched your life, but you will also be compelled to look to the future with a deep desire to make whatever years remain effective and relevant.

Jim Graham
Gold Hill Baptist Church

CHAPTER ONE

For This We Have Jesus

For the joys and for the sorrows,
The best and worst of times;
For this moment, for tomorrow,
For all that lies behind.
Fears that crowd around me;
For the failure of my plans;
For the dreams of all I hope to be,
The truth of what I am—

For the tears that flow in secret
In the broken times;
For the moments of elation,
Or the troubled mind;
For all the disappointments
Or the sting of old regrets;
All my prayers and longings
That seem unanswered yet—

For the weakness of my body,
The burdens of each day;
For the nights of doubt and worry
When sleep has fled away;
Needing reassurance
And the will to start again,
A steely-eyed endurance,
The strength to fight and win—

For this I have Jesus,
For this I have Jesus,
For this I have Jesus,
I have Jesus.

Graham Kendrick
Copyright © 1994 Make Way Music, P.O. Box 263,
Croydon, Surrey CR9 5AP UK.
All rights reserved. International copyright secured.
Used by permission.

It was the Easter of 1995 and I was at Spring Harvest—the great Christian holiday festival of teaching and praise—as a speaker. Exactly two years before I had been at the same meeting with my husband Roy, thanking the crowds of Christians there for all their support and the loving messages they had sent during his illness. This year I was there alone, because in September 1994 Roy died from lung cancer.

I was aware of the atmosphere of excitement and anticipation all around me as I made my way to the platform to join the other speakers, ready for the main evening meeting to begin. I looked out over the marquee full of over six thousand people, and my mouth went dry. I had been asked to lead them in a short prayer, and I was terrified! I am quite happy to talk about my faith to any size of group for any length of time, but I didn't feel that I could pray in front of such a huge crowd for a single minute. And I was sitting with such well-known Christians—Roger and Faith Forster were there, and Steve Gaukroger, Luis Palau and Graham Kendrick. I felt very small and inadequate. 'Lord, help me,' I prayed silently. 'Give me your words.'

As I prayed, Graham Kendrick began to sing a new song which he had just written, and the words reached me through the waves of my panic: 'For this I have Jesus.' Roger Forster leaned over and tapped me on the arm.

'Did you hear how Graham came to write this, Fiona?'

he asked. 'Charles Price was preaching and told the story of an elderly friend of his who always said "For this I have Jesus"—it was his catchphrase, and he used it on every occasion, and for everything that happened to him, good or bad! Graham heard it and it inspired him to write this song.'

As the chorus swelled around me, and six thousand voices joined in the words, I knew how I should pray, and my nervousness drained away. I got to my feet. 'I don't know all of you people here tonight,' I began, 'but Jesus does. He knows you by name, and he knows all the joys and sorrows, and all the circumstances of your life. I don't know how you have come here tonight, or what your burdens are, but I do know that whatever we are carrying, we can lay it before Jesus in perfect confidence. This is why he came—to let us know that we have a loving Father in heaven who cares for us. "He was despised and rejected by men, a man of sorrows and familiar with suffering." He understands all our feelings, so we can turn to him in trust. "For this we have Jesus."'

The prayer I prayed after that was short, but it was heartfelt, because that was the lesson that God had been teaching me through all the weary months of Roy's illness, and now after his death I was still proving it to be true.

In the spring and summer of 1992 Roy had been through chemotherapy and radiotherapy in an attempt to eradicate his cancer. However, in spite of the delight of the specialists that the tumour had disappeared from the X-ray, the final checkup had been inconclusive: there were still some cancer cells present in his lung. It remained to be seen whether they would grow again, so we lived with the knowledge that they might and with the hope that they wouldn't. Roy seemed to be restored to perfect health, though, and went back to a full schedule of work for nearly a year—a very happy year which we lived and enjoyed to the full. Every healthy day was a bonus.

During the summer of 1993 Roy was performing with Harry Secombe in *Pickwick* at the Chichester Festival Theatre—a prestigious and delightful theatre to work. He enjoyed every moment of it; with Harry topping the bill, the company was bound to be a happy one. Roy had known and loved Harry for many years and had always looked to him as a role model for keeping your feet firmly on the ground in show business! In 1965 Roy had played Sam Weller in the New York production of *Pickwick*—the difference this time was that he was playing Sam Weller's father!

However, during the run Roy developed a persistent cough which neither antibiotics nor asthma treatments seemed able to clear, and we began the cycle of tests and visits to doctors once more. By the end of November he was in great pain and unable to swallow properly, and it became clear that the cancer had returned. This time the specialist was gloomy.

'The prognosis is poorer this time,' he said. 'The cancer has started up again, and we can't subject you to treatment of such intensity again. My advice is to go home and enjoy Christmas.'

Nevertheless he prescribed some chemotherapy pills and Roy's determined spirit took over. He took the pills and insisted on fulfilling his promise and opening in *Pickwick* which was playing for the Christmas season in Birmingham.

We chose a hotel next door to the theatre, and I went with him to do the driving and to nurse him if necessary.

One problem was the difficulty Roy had in swallowing solid food—I knew that he couldn't manage normal hotel meals. What we needed was a room with a fridge where I could keep supplies of liquidised fruit and other drinks ready for him. The Forte Crest Hotel in Birmingham accepted this odd request without a murmur, but I was unprepared for what they provided for us. We arrived tired and tense—I was still unsure that the whole enterprise was a wise one in Roy's state of health—and when I opened the door I stood still for a moment and then burst into tears. They had given us a whole suite (for the price of a double room!) and had transformed a small storage room into a mini kitchen, with a fridge, a kettle, a microwave and a cooker. Two workmen had worked through the night to get it ready for Roy. The room was filled with fruit and flowers, and nothing could have better expressed the affection in which Roy was held, and the respect people had for his indomitable spirit in fighting his cancer in full view of everyone.

Both the cast of *Pickwick* and the public were immensely supportive, and Roy's part had been cut down so that he would not get too tired. Usually he catnapped in the dressing room between his entrances, and on one occasion he awoke with a start to hear the backstage tannoy calling 'Roy Castle on stage now!' Terrified of missing his cue Roy jumped up still half asleep, hit every wall of the dressing room and then walked into a closed door! The chemotherapy pills often left him confused, and when he forgot his lines he just made them up until the other members of the cast dragged him back to the script. I think they all enjoyed the diversions, and they certainly helped him along with great good humour.

We had a strange Christmas that year. The specialist

had told us to gather all the family together, as he thought that Roy was unlikely to live into the New Year. However, Roy was managing much better than anyone had expected, so we decided not to call our daughter Julia back from Peru. She was due home for a holiday in February anyway. The rest of us enjoyed ourselves, and as Roy was working until the day before Christmas Eve I was unable to do any preparation. I just called in at Marks and Spencer, bought an entirely instant Christmas dinner, packed it into the car and drove it home! It was a remarkably restful time.

After Christmas we returned to Birmingham for the rest of the run. Roy was still taking a variety of medicines for his cough, but as none of them seemed to have much effect, in the end he decided to stop taking anything at all. Unfortunately the last medication had been methadone, the drug used to wean addicts off heroin, and neither of us realised that Roy was now effectively addicted to it. Suddenly stopping it was like an addict going 'cold turkey', but we failed to recognise the symptoms. He suffered from terrible insomnia and claustrophobia, and spent the nights pacing restlessly around the hotel room. Often I would wake up and keep him company, making him drinks, chatting or watching TV, and just trying to make him comfortable. One night, while I was asleep, he stood looking out over the balcony to the silent street, nine floors below. In that moment, he told me later, he was tempted to step off and escape his suffering. I knew he was very ill but I had no idea that he was feeling suicidal, and I felt dreadful when he told me. Fortunately he rejected that way out, because of the suffering it would cause the rest of us, but I was grieved that I had been asleep that night.

15

He was determined not to give in and leave *Pickwick*, however ill he felt, so when we were told that the show was closing unexpectedly it was shocking but welcome news. The theatre had gone bankrupt, which meant that it had to cease trading immediately—the run ended with a matinée performance and that was that. In fact Roy was so ill that evening that I was really worried about driving him home to Gerrards Cross; I was mentally planning escape routes on the way, in case we had to stop and find a hospital.

Once again we visited the doctor, and once again medication was prescribed which seemed to put things right for a time. We were back on the old switchback of treatment, with improvements and side-effects swinging us up and down. However, we always felt that God was our secret weapon. The doctors, for all their expertise, care and concern, did not include God in their calculations; we did. We never claimed miracles, nor did we ever claim that Roy was or would be healed. We simply said that we could trust God whatever the circumstances; here were the circumstances back again, and we were still trusting.

Roy had been a committed Christian for many years but he had never felt the need to be baptised; as he put it, he and God had a perfectly good understanding, and it didn't need to be put on public display. I had chosen to be baptised in 1981, about four years after we moved to Gold Hill Baptist Church, though the church itself did not require this—it was left entirely up to members to decide for themselves. Nevertheless it was encouraged, and some of our friends clearly would have liked to see Roy choose adult baptism. In fact he had been 'christened' as an adult in order to be confirmed in the Anglican church before we were married.

'How many times do I have to go through this?' he asked me one day. 'Surely the creed says, "I acknowledge one baptism for the remission of sins"?' The more people pressed, cajoled and hinted, the more resolute he became, and I could see his hackles go up every time it was mentioned.

'If I ever get baptised by total immersion it will be because God tells me, not because other people tell me,' he said. 'Besides, I don't want to be an exhibitionist and have people think I'm doing it to draw attention to myself.'

I could see the difficult position he was in—he was scared that the press would find out and make a publicity stunt out of it. He even thought about the possibility of being baptised in a swimming pool with just a few friends around!

However, eventually he decided that he wanted everything God had available for him—he didn't want to miss out on anything. If baptism was part of God's will, then he was willing to go along with it. The perfect time came when Julia was home from Peru, and Daniel and his wife Birthe were visiting. Antonia and Benjamin were living at home so we were all together for the simple ceremony at Gold Hill. He was the only one to be baptised that evening, but he was so keen to keep it a secret that though the baptismal pool was open and ready, no one knew why until he got up and walked forward.

The hymn he had chosen was 'Be bold, be strong', which he joked was to be interpreted as 'Be bald, be strong', as the chemotherapy had once again robbed him of his hair. At the end, everyone broke into spontaneous applause, delighted that he had wanted to make this public declaration of his faith. It was a joyful occasion, and Roy said that he felt a tremendous calm as he emerged from the water to face his future.

We had no idea, of course, how long that future was likely to be, but Roy always pointed out that neither did any of us; all life is uncertain. Roy was certain, though, that whatever time he had left was to be used to the glory of God. He felt sure that God still had some purpose for him, and he was ready and eager to do whatever was in his will.

One project to which he had already pledged his support was 'Cause for Hope'—an ambitious appeal to establish a lung cancer research centre. We had met Ray Donnelly, a cardiothoracic surgeon at the Broadgreen Hospital in Liverpool and Chairman of the Lung Cancer Fund, who was enthusiastically championing the cause; he felt that it was vital to have funds targeted specially at this common cancer. He wanted to sponsor research into the genetic and environmental causes of lung cancer and work towards its early diagnosis, treatment and prevention. Knowing that Roy was willing to be open about his own battle with the disease, Ray felt that he was the ideal person to front the appeal. Roy agreed to lend his name to the project, but pointed out that as he was already very sick he would be unable to do much personally.

Roy launched the appeal in Birmingham and Liverpool; as the centre was to be built in Liverpool the 'Scouse' welcome was amazing! We were invited to Anfield to the final 'Derby' between Liverpool and Everton before the Kop was demolished. Roy was asked to toss the coin before the kick-off, and a bucket collection was taken. It was Mothering Sunday, and I couldn't resist asking Roy, 'Is this supposed to be my Mother's Day treat?' but he was blissfully happy, and so proud, especially when the crowds in the Kop began singing 'There's only one Roy Castle.'

In between fund-raising he was working again: *Pickwick* was on tour in Sheffield and Norwich, and later he toured with an Old Time Music Hall show. During the tour of *Pickwick*, Harry Secombe had suggested to Roy that he should write his autobiography, and when he seemed diffident, had introduced him to his publisher, Jeremy Robson. It was a miracle that the deadline he was given for completing the manuscript was the end of June 1994—Roy's technique was always 'just' to meet deadlines, and had it been any later the book (called *Now and Then*) would not have been completed. As it was, he had to allow his editor to insert last-minute thoughts and additions from his diary, and to choose from the many photographs he had accumulated over the years.

It wasn't until May that the next phase of the illness declared itself. We had travelled to Manchester to speak at a Christian meeting, and were sitting around a dining table with some other guests. Roy was idly drumming his two index fingers on the edge of the table to some private beat inside his head, when he became aware that his left hand felt rather sluggish. He kept up with the cheerful conversation around the table, but from time to time he tested his fingers; there was no doubt that his left hand wasn't working properly. He told me quietly so as not to alarm the other guests; my stomach lurched but I managed to keep smiling.

'There's probably a logical explanation for it,' I assured him in an undertone. 'Perhaps you're tired. It'll be all right tomorrow.' But as we drove home that night our hearts were heavy. Roy recalled a story he had heard about George Gershwin: one day he suddenly found his fingers stumbling over an arpeggio he had always played easily; he died shortly afterwards of a brain tumour.

We had been warned that cancer patients often developed secondary tumours; with lung cancer, the secondary sites were often in the brain. An urgent visit to the specialist confirmed that a scan showed two brain tumours, and we knew that the treatment available was very limited. We were looking down a tunnel into the future, and the end began to seem in sight. I prayed that Roy might be spared too much suffering, but even in my anguish I felt that God had not deserted us. I recalled that when Roy's cancer was first diagnosed I had felt that God was saying to us, 'Stand back and see what I will do through this.' Now I was sure he was telling us, 'It isn't finished yet.' God still had work for both of us to do.

CHAPTER TWO

Journey's End

———————

For the joys and for the sorrows,
The best and worst of times;
For this moment, for tomorrow,
For all that lies behind—

The Cause for Hope Appeal had been launched in January 1994 in Birmingham and Liverpool. Roy had attended various functions after that to raise funds, but the big event was planned for the summer: a Tour of Hope, by train, covering 1,200 miles and visiting eight major cities. All these plans had been made in the knowledge that Roy's cancer had returned, but without knowing quite how ill he would be by July.

Shortly before the tour was due to start, Roy was once again having increasing trouble in swallowing, difficulty in breathing, and generally feeling very unwell, so the specialist arranged an endoscopy—a procedure carried out while the patient is under sedation, when a tiny camera is lowered down the throat to enable the doctor to see inside. It showed that there was no tumour in Roy's oesophagus, but that the tumour on his lung was pressing on his gullet, giving him a sensation that there was always a lump just below his throat. The cancer was so advanced by this stage that all the doctors could do was to try to make him more comfortable, so they increased the dose of morphine to allow him to rest while they completed their tests. That evening I drove him to London where he performed in cabaret!

Soon afterwards, though, his breathing difficulties increased, and he was admitted to hospital again. One evening at around 9 pm the specialist rang me at home. He said that Roy had been telling him, with great enthusiasm, about the Tour of Hope. I was absolutely amazed. I hadn't dared to mention the idea to the doctors in case they laughed at me: it was so obvious that Roy was a very sick man, not one who was about to undertake a gruelling fund-raising tour!

'Really?' I answered hesitantly. 'I didn't mention it because I couldn't imagine he'd be well enough to do it. I've advised the fund-raisers to make contingency plans. It looks as though we'll have to cancel the whole thing.'

'Don't dismiss the idea,' the specialist replied. 'We have ways of patching people up well enough to let them have their final request—only I have to say that it's usually a world cruise, not a train trip round England! I think you'll find we can make him comfortable enough to try it, at least. It seems to mean a lot to him.'

'It does,' I replied. 'It's a charity that's very close to his heart for obvious reasons—and he promised he'd do it—and he does so hate to let people down.'

When I visited Roy in hospital the next day he was still keen to go on with the tour, in spite of the fact that the heavy sedative he had been given was making him sound slightly drunk. We went for a mad walk around the hospital grounds together, with Roy walking sideways like a crab, and both of us giggling helplessly at the funny sight we must be.

It wasn't really a laughing matter, of course. Roy needed large doses of morphine to control his pain, and sometimes these made him confused and caused his speech to be slurred. The nurses had warned me that already they had been trying to keep the press away, and we knew that when Roy left the hospital they would be there with cameras at the hospital door. I wanted to protect him from this sort of intrusion, but at the same time I knew that we had always been as open as we could about all aspects of his illness. In the end I went outside first and spoke to the assembled reporters.

'Look,' I said, 'I'm taking Roy home now. Why don't you all go home to our house and wait in the drive? Then we can get home and Roy can settle in, and then you can have your interviews.'

They did as I asked, and we went home quietly. Then Roy sat in a chair and gave the interviews—including one for Sky News—as we had planned. I had warned the reporters that he had had a large dose of morphine, because I didn't want anyone to ridicule his slow, slurred speech, but I need not have worried: as always, Roy responded to the cameras and gave a competent performance.

When he was asked why he was raising funds for something that would obviously come to fruition too late to benefit himself, he replied that there were 40,000 people in Great Britain suffering from lung cancer. 'It's as if I'm pulling on a rope, and there are all those people behind me pulling too. We want to find a cure for this disease, so I can't let them down. I have to say, "All right back there, chaps?" and we go on pulling together.'

The next day we drove to GMTV for yet another interview. For the first time in my life with Roy I had asserted myself and insisted on sitting beside him during the interview. Normally I would have run a mile from such a suggestion, but it's amazing how strong you can be on behalf of someone else. I felt that I needed to be his brain, so that if he couldn't remember something (which often happened lately) I could chip in and cover up for him. I didn't want him to look silly in front of the cameras. However, once again he applied all his available energy to the task in hand and I sat mute, feeling like a lemon sitting purposelessly beside him.

From the studio we went on to Euston to meet the train that was to take us north. Roy met all the requests of the photographers, posing by the train, and even blowing a guard's whistle and waving a green flag. There was another exhausting round of interviews, and at one point he came very close to passing out. I was all prepared and was supposed to administer the next dose of morphine, but didn't dare give it to him in case he started talking rubbish. More publicity photographs were taken with Sir John and Lady Mills, who were also supporting the Appeal, and at last we were able to board the train. From then on we decided that he would give one major interview with all the press present at once, to save his energy.

By now Roy was so ill that he was not strong enough to walk the length of the train to our sleeping compartment, but just rested in an ordinary seat. I was tremendously relieved to meet Pauline Murphy, the Millington nurse and a trained cancer specialist, kindly organised for us by Ray Donnelly, who was joining us for the trip. She would be able to give Roy the medication he needed, and to assess the situation and tell us whenever he was doing too much.

We spent that night in Liverpool, where we were given the most tremendous welcome. Many show-business friends were performing in a variety show at the Liverpool Empire called 'For the Love of Roy' in aid of the Appeal, and Cliff Richard spoke movingly in a televised interview about Roy's faith and his dedication to helping other people. Roy was not well enough to perform, but at the end he walked with help to the middle of the stage, where he received a standing ovation that had to be seen to be believed. As it died down he said, with typical humour, 'Is that all?' Later on he commented, 'I used not to get that much applause after I'd worked my guts out for an hour in cabaret. Now I get it for just making it to the centre of the stage!'

The next day we set off early to do the press conference and TV and radio interviews on Lime Street Station. Crowds were filling the station area, which otherwise would have been deserted since there was a one-day rail strike. The signalmen had actually offered to go to work for free, just to see our train through, but Roy felt that we should not have any special treatment. Not to be defeated, we had been loaned the Liverpool FC coach, which drove us to each destination we would have reached by train. At one point Roy collapsed and had to rest on the special train which was waiting for us, and then he was 'go-carted' from train to coach.

We departed amid waves and cheers and brass bands and mounted police, towards our next stop—Manchester. Once there, Roy was too ill to get off the coach to do a walkabout, so I stayed with him on the coach to protect him from well-meaning inquirers. Our next stop was Huddersfield, specially chosen because it was Roy's birth-place and an area for which he had tremendous affection and wonderful memories. I woke him up a few times as we were driving across the moors: the views were magni-ficent and I was aware that this might be his last glimpse of his beloved Yorkshire. He was glad to be woken and mouthed the word 'home' with a warm smile.

There was a wonderful welcome awaiting him in the Square, and he watched from his window as children sang and danced for him. Many old friends had turned up and I had to ask them to go onto the bus to greet him; I could tell that he was fed up with himself for not being able to rise to the occasion, but he did his best.

His health continued to deteriorate that day: by the time we arrived in Newcastle his face was flushed with fever and he began being sick into a bucket. Simon Bates had volunteered to join us on the trip so that he could help with just such occasions as this; he was already out among the crowds telling them to gather round the coach and that Roy would come to the door to speak to them. There was nothing else to be done, so in my sternest voice I told Roy to stop being sick, pull himself together and get to the door because people were waiting for him, and he did just that!

Later on a group of girls from *Byker Grove* came on board to talk to Roy and they were all in tears. It was very touching to see these young people so affected by his condition—we didn't have to guess at what was going on in their minds.

At this point someone made the decision to divert us to the airport, where a plane belonging to Littlewoods would take us directly to Glasgow. I had never flown in a six-seater plane before. I would have enjoyed it more if I had not been so concerned about Roy: every bump and roll seemed to make him worse, and there was nothing I could do.

He was exhausted by the travelling and the effort he had put into smiling, chatting and thanking people for their generous help and donations to the fund. That night in the hotel I was really afraid that he was going to die. Even Pauline, our nurse, admitted that she wasn't sure that he was going to make it. Somehow we were all being fuelled by Roy's indomitable courage and his determination to do something tremendous to raise funds for other sufferers.

I sat in the sitting room of our suite (all the accom-modation had been donated by well-wishers to enable the trip to happen) and prayed. A whole series of concerns was buzzing around in my head. I was aware that the journey was probably hastening Roy's death, and that I was contributing by going along with it. I was concerned that the trip would degrade Roy, by allowing him to appear either daft, because of the drugs, or ill and seeming to call for pity. And I wondered whether people would get the wrong idea, and think that the trip was being undertaken from the wrong motives—for self-aggrandisement and publicity for its own sake, rather than the publicity needed desperately for fund-raising in a good cause.

I can remember staring out of the window at the twinkling lights of the city, and thinking what a bleak place the world looked. Roy was going through terrible pain, and I was powerless to help him. My mind was racing, trying to decide whether we should abandon the whole plan and fly home where he could get treatment.

'Are we wrong to do this, Jesus?' I prayed. 'Should I persuade Roy to give up and go home? What should I do?'

As I prayed I felt peace steal into my heart. Words from the Bible came into my mind so clearly that I knew God was speaking to me through them: 'Greater love hath no man than this, that he lay down his life for his friends.' Of course! Roy himself would get no benefit from this—his concern that other people would have a better chance of treatment and recovery. I was able to relax, and trust in God's fatherly love for us, and in his purposes. I was reminded again of the words that had come to me when the first diagnosis of cancer was made: 'Stand back, and see what I am going to do through this.' I was filled with admiration for Roy's spirit in taking on this trip, and I was sure that it was God's will that he would get through it—somehow.

The next morning Roy sat up in bed and said, 'OK, let's get going!' I set off ahead of him to the city centre for a photo call and to meet some young tap dancers; I even managed a few rusty time steps in my trainers for the benefit of the press. Roy joined us later at the station in the tender care of Pauline—it felt a bit like having a nanny!

A show had been planned to take place in Argyll Street in Glasgow, but Roy was too weak to leave the train, so the show came to him and we watched from the platform. Simon Bates said in a TV interview at the time that he was finding it increasingly difficult to cope with what was going on. Time after time he saw Roy absolutely exhausted—the chemotherapy drained him of energy— yet whenever there was a show to watch, a child to thank, a group of people who had come to see him, he would make a supreme effort of will and summon up the energy from somewhere to shake hands, crack a joke, and let people know how much he appreciated their efforts to help. Simon himself was wonderful—he always knew just how to command attention in the nicest way, and kept everybody organised.

On Friday we visited Bristol, Plymouth and Cardiff before returning to Waterloo. We were met by a crowd of friends and well-wishers, and we unveiled the name-plate on a locomotive which had been specially named: Roy Castle OBE. I have never had any interest in train spotting, but when I travel these days I find myself looking at every engine to see if it is Roy's. Once I was standing on Reading station late at night, and there it was! I wanted to shout to everyone, but instead just stood in silence as all those emotions and memories came flooding back.

Magician Paul Daniels was interviewed on the station, just before he handed over a large cheque for the Appeal from the Water Rats. He, too, admired Roy's courage in persevering with the tour.

'I've just been talking to his doctor,' he said, 'and the doctor says he doesn't know what he's running on. Whenever there's an appearance to be made, this guy just comes through. The doctors doubted if he'd be able to walk off the train: he walked off the train. He just finds a reserve of energy from somewhere.'

It was this stubborn refusal to give in to exhaustion and pain, and this willingness to smile and joke and be cheerful in the face of his illness, which so impressed people. Even the porters who carried our bags off the train reached into their pockets and put handfuls of change into the collecting buckets.

We had visited eight cities in four days. It was a punishing schedule by anyone's standards; for a sick man it was ridiculous. Yet at every stop Roy managed to leave the train, even if he had to sit in a wheelchair to move a few yards down the platform. And the money poured in. By the time we reached London it was clear that in four days Roy had raised over a million pounds towards the building of the research centre. He was weak and in pain, and we were both exhausted, but elated because we had succeeded in what we had set out to do. Roy had not only helped the Cause for Hope Appeal; he had also cheered and encouraged countless other cancer sufferers.

Three days later he went into hospital for an operation to help his eating difficulty: the surgeon inserted a rigid tube into his oesophagus, so that the tumour could not compress it. The operation left him weaker than ever, and the specialist warned me that Roy might not last the night. Our elder daughter Julia was still working in Peru, but I called the rest of the children together. They all arrived at the hospital around 5 pm and stood around the bed, uncertain of what they should do; Roy seemed to be unconscious. Dan took Roy's hand and said softly, 'I love you, Dad,' and burst into tears. That finished us all off, and we all turned away, crying quietly. Suddenly a gruff voice said, 'What's the matter with you all?' and made us all laugh. Roy had opened his eyes onto the classic death-bed scene, and as usual played for a laugh. Once again, against all expectation, he rallied and made some sort of recovery. He wasn't ready to die yet—he would be coming home.

An extract from my diary for 29th July:

After fitful, uncomfortable and exhausted sleep I woke very early about 4.45 and made myself a drink in the staff kitchen at the hospital. I sat drinking it and praying the Lord's Prayer. Then Roy woke. I gave him a drink and wished him a happy 31st Wedding Anniversary, and thanked him for all the years of joy and happiness and love he had given me. I didn't have a card or a present for him, but a heart which over all the years had been and always would be his.

I opened the window wide to allow the fresh morning air to fill the room. The stillness and beauty of the hospital gardens gave me such peace . . . I prayed for my family. I released them once again to God. I relinquished my right once again to everything. All that is in God's hands. I put on, on behalf of us all, God's armour to stand against the enemy's invasion. The helmet of salvation; the breastplate of righteousness—his righteousness; the strong belt of truth—his truth; shoes to speed me on to preach the gospel of peace, by living it rather than by shouting it.

This reminded me of a letter we had received which told us to show the world 'how a Christian should die'. It had not troubled me but posed questions in my mind: what did this man want us to do? Go through a performance of dying to satisfy his desires? No, I saw that in living and in dying we are Christ's, and what man perceives is not our problem. Alleluia for the release of that responsibility. God was not placing that burden on us . . .

The birds were now singing and finding their breakfasts on the lawn . . . everything has its season, God's perfection for us, his timing in our lives. His numbering of our days, nothing to fear, nothing to weep for. Just pure joy in my heart for all the blessings he had so faithfully and so richly given to us through all our days.

During the time Roy was in hospital I often had time to pray and meditate, and I was grateful for the opportunity; I knew that the time of testing was ahead of us. Roy was discharged after five days, and came home to Gerrards Cross. I knew that I was going to be nursing him from now on. He was fully aware that he was dying, and our time together was all the more precious. He was in a great deal of pain, and I would often stay up all night to give him his medication and talk to him when he was wakeful.

Sometimes we both felt very low and weary of the whole business of suffering; at other times we were uplifted by the support of friends and the comfort of the Holy Spirit. On 5th August I wrote in my diary:

On Monday August 1st when Roy came out of hospital he was very low. When we prayed he said that he felt God had abandoned him and he couldn't feel him anywhere. I felt the same and was very despondent because I couldn't give him any reassurance. Later during the week with this question on my mind I started to think that even if I doubted the Lord, I had nowhere else to go but to him. I know for a certainty that nothing and no one else could meet my needs, or speak truth, or help me, but the Lord. I could hide nowhere. I have been reading the Psalms—many times the psalmist expresses lone-liness, abandonment and desperation. I realise in our human-ness we are not alone. This gave me such reassurance . . .

6th August

During the past couple of days Roy has been seeing 'inde-scribable bright lights'. He also expressed 'hearing' the song 'Because He lives, I can face tomorrow' which gave him real reassurance. Today we had a beautiful time of Communion. I was reminded of Romans 8: Nothing can separate us from the love of God. Roy then prayed: 'O God, thank you for the gift of your Son—such grace . . .' It was so moving to hear him pray so fervently when I had thought he was asleep.

7th August

Roy had a very bad night—distressed, in pain and vomiting all through the night—the pain was heightened because of the tube, so we didn't get much sleep. By morning he was very weak with irregular breathing and his eyes were rolling backwards occasionally. I really thought that this was it. I dressed quickly and sat with him holding his hand, telling him I loved him. He asked me to kiss him, his voice an almost inaudible whisper. He told me that he had always loved me and that nothing had ever made him change his mind.

After a while a big smile came over his face and he said 'Oh, yes, it's just beautiful, so soft, so warm. The pain—it's still there but it's so comfortable. There's nothing to worry about.'

I was crying, but I would have been so happy had Jesus come for him then. But he gradually started getting stronger and the pain returned . . .

Antonia and Benjamin are both away. Roy had a bad night, and we were whispering together when I suddenly said, 'Why are we whispering? We're alone in the house, we can party!'

'Isn't it amazing?' said Roy. 'If we were Jewish we'd have the whole family wailing at the bedside, but as it is we've been abandoned!'

33

9th August

Sitting at Roy's bedside I saw a smile spreading across his face—this after a night and day of vomiting and great pain. I went over and asked why the smile. He whispered back almost inaudibly, 'It's beautiful . . . the most wonderful gardens. What a gardener! I thought I was a gardener, but this gardener's something else.' I asked him if the pain was gone and he said no, but about half of it was gone. 'It's so lovely—don't hang about, darling! I don't know that I'm going to die yet, but I've got to be patient.'

As the days wore on, Roy's pain became more intense, and the dose of morphine he was taking had to be raised. In the end the doctor fitted him with a syringe 'driver' which administers a regular dose of the medication every two minutes, and can be boosted whenever necessary. Towards the end of the month Rob and Di Parsons came for a visit, and they could see clearly the change in Roy, especially in his decreasing awareness. At times he was perfectly lucid, but much of the time he was sleepy, or in a world of his own when he could not really respond to conversation.

One night he remembered that he wanted to sign the first copy of his autobiography (which had arrived a few days before) and give it to Jim Graham, our pastor. So he lay in bed at 3.45 am, patiently trying to practise his signature. If only we'd had a video camera! In the end he managed a signature he was happy with, and went peacefully back to sleep.

I still could not decide whether to tell Julia to come home—so often Roy had seemed on the brink of death, only to rally once more. Roy was well enough to speak to her on the phone himself, and he told her, 'If you want to come home for your own benefit, then come. If you're thinking of coming because of me, don't—I don't want to disrupt your life.' Julia thanked him, went to the travel agent, and took the first flight home.

By the time she arrived Roy was scarcely able to speak, but he was able to recognise her, for which I was profoundly grateful. He even remembered where she had been. For the first day, every time she came into the room he would smile broadly and whisper, 'Julia! Peru!'

Julia later wrote about that journey home:

I wasn't sure what to expect when I got there: I imagined someone coming to the airport and saying I was too late—that he'd already died. That would have been awful—he would have thought I didn't care. Dan and Birthe picked me up from the airport and started explaining Dad's condition. It made me cry. It was difficult to imagine him not being in control.

It was such a relief when I got home and he recognised me, but it was very hard, seeing him in that state: the others had been watching a gradual deterioration, but for me it was a real shock. He could still make us all laugh, though: when I walked into the room for the first time, he was so surprised to see me that he tried to get out of bed. We asked him what he was doing and he said he was going to the gobsmackler shop!

I had been so busy in Peru that I hadn't realised how important for my own peace of mind it was for me to be there. At one point Dad looked round at us all and said, 'Oh—we were waiting for someone, weren't we? We don't have to wait any more.' That meant a lot to me, as it showed he knew I was there.

Those last few days were very difficult, and I was glad to have the family around us. We were bombarded by constant phone calls and mail—kind thoughts by well-wishers, but all requiring time and energy I wanted to keep for Roy. There was a telephone in the bedroom, but

I kept the bell switched off so that it would not disturb him, and left the answerphone on during the day.

One evening, however, I was talking to Ray Donnelly on the phone in the room. Roy was making awful choking noises, as he was too ill and sedated to cough and clear his lungs, and Ray could hear the sound of his tortured breathing down the phone. 'What can I do?' I asked Ray, tearfully. 'I can't help him and I don't know what to do.' Ray asked me a few questions about how much medication Roy was taking, and reassured me. 'It's much worse for you than it is for him, Fiona. Believe me, he isn't aware of the state he's in.' I chose to believe him then, but I knew that the end must be very near. It was the 31st August—Roy's sixty-second birthday.

For his birthday we had made an ice-cream cake—the only thing that would slip down his throat. When we sang Happy Birthday he smiled and whispered 'Happy Birthday,' and seemed to know what was happening. There had been many tributes to him in the media, and we took a radio into his room for the Gloria Hunniford Show: she played 'Good Morning' from the show *Singing in the Rain*, a song which Roy and Tommy Steele had danced to. Roy followed it very carefully, as if remembering the steps, and when it was over he said thoughtfully, 'That was very difficult.' They were his last real words.

On the last night I sat up beside him as his breathing grew shallower and his pulse weaker, and I knew that at last the battle was over. I didn't want to disturb the children, so I lay down on the bed beside him and held his hand, and felt his spirit slip away. He died at 5.15 on the morning of Friday 2nd September, free at last of pain and suffering, and went home to the Lord Jesus whom he had loved and followed for so long.

CHAPTER THREE

Saying Goodbye

Fears that crowd around me,
For the failure of my plans;
For the dreams of all I hope to be,
The truth of what I am—

Strangely, on the morning that Roy died I had the distinct impression that his spirit had left his body about an hour before he finally stopped breathing. I was tired after my many nights of nursing and yet I felt quite calm. I had been expecting this for so long, and my overwhelming feeling was relief that his suffering was over. I lay beside him for a few moments longer, and then I got up and opened the curtains. It was almost dawn, and the sky was growing lighter, but I felt it was still too early to wake the family. I went downstairs and made myself a pot of tea, then I came back to look after Roy for the last time.

I washed him and tidied the bed, and packed away the syringe driver that had delivered the morphine. Then I thought, I'm going to have a busy day today, so I went and washed my hair.

It seems odd to me now, but I suppose I was operating on a sort of auto-pilot in which my practical nature took over and suggested the next activity. It seems to be a common reaction—I remember a neighbour telephoning me to tell me that her husband had died; I rushed round at once, to find her putting on her make-up and doing her hair. Her comment was, 'Well, the doctor will be here in a minute!'

At about seven o'clock I made more drinks and took trays up to the bedrooms, woke the children and told them that Roy had died. They all came in to our bedroom and we prayed together round the bed. No one was sobbing aloud, but we were all very emotional and weepy.

Then I turned to Benjamin and said, 'What are you going to do about Blackpool?'

It was the day when the Blackpool illuminations were to be switched on. Shirley Bassey was going to throw the switch, and then hand over a cheque for the Cause for Hope Appeal. Ben was planning to be there anyway, with the National Youth Jazz Orchestra, and he was supposed to receive the cheque on Roy's behalf. If he went, he would have to leave the house at 9 am.

'Why don't you go and pray about it for a while?' I suggested. Ben hesitated for a moment, and then said, almost at once, 'I'll go. I know Dad would want me to.'

I was very proud of him. He told me later that when he got on the coach which was taking the orchestra to Blackpool, he told everyone at once that Roy had died. He thought it would be easier than to have each one in turn asking him how his father was. In fact, the whole group was immensely supportive. By the time they arrived in Blackpool the news of Roy's death had broken, and outside the place where they were playing a newspaper hoarding bore the words 'Roy Castle is dead'. Two of his friends tore the paper off the sign—a kind act of vandalism as they didn't want Ben to see such a stark statement.

Meanwhile, back in Gerrards Cross, I decided that the next job was to find an undertaker. The husband of our church caretaker had died fairly recently, so I knew that she would know how to go about it. I went down to the church to see her. I was fine until I started telling her why I had come, but then I broke down and cried as she hugged me. Graham Dawson, one of the pastors of our church, was leading a men's morning prayer meeting. He offered to contact the undertaker for me, so I went home and started on my list of people to ring. At the top was our doctor, of course, and he promised to come to the house at about 10 am after his surgery and write the death certificate.

Telling other people was a delicate matter. I had to keep saying to them, 'Please keep this quiet until I've had a chance to contact all the family,' because I wanted to tell them myself, and not have them find out at second hand through the media. As usual, I was wary of the press finding out too soon; once they knew, everything would become public, so I knew I had to be careful and organised in what I did. Even the undertaker was told to come 'in an unmarked van'—like a spy!—so that no one would find out by accident.

I was still at the phone, working through my list, at lunchtime. Inevitably, though, there was a slip. I rang one show-business friend who happened to speak to his agent five minutes later; the agent contacted a reporter and the story was out. I was irritated because I hadn't yet managed to track down my sister, and she heard of Roy's death from someone else—exactly the situation I had been trying so hard to avoid.

One person who had been near the top of my list was Roy's agent; of course the reporters descended on him as soon as they knew. He rang me to warn me that the press were on their way, and said that they were bound to want a statement from me. I said the first thing that came into my head: 'No flowers, no fuss, no mourning, just lots of joy.'

'That's great,' he replied. 'That'll do.' And he put down the phone. Ten minutes later the newsreader on

ITN's lunchtime news announced Roy's death and repeated the words I had said.

Half an hour later two TV crews arrived at the house, from Carlton and Sky News. I told them to set up their equipment on the patio and I would come out and see them. Alison Jack had brought me a beautiful bouquet of flowers; she had interviewed us several times before during Roy's illness, and she was clearly upset at having to intrude on us at this time. I felt very sorry for her, being put in such an awkward position, and I wanted to make them all feel more comfortable about it. So I gave the interviews and was as normal as possible, and managed to make them laugh and relax. Then I got the giggles, because I didn't seem to be behaving much like a grieving widow, worrying about whether I'd made enough coffee for an army of cameramen and trying to cheer everyone up.

After the television crews came the newspaper reporters, so I took them into the sitting room out of the way. At about one o'clock the undertaker came (in his plain van as arranged) to take away Roy's body. Daniel came into the room, closing the door behind him, and raised his eyebrows meaningfully at me. There was a tremendous banging and bumping as the coffin was manoeuvred with difficulty round the narrow turn in the stairs. I was desperately speaking more and more loudly over the top of all this, and trying to keep them all talking until the coast was clear—I did not want pictures of Roy's coffin in the papers.

The phone was ringing constantly, and I was very glad that my first instinct had been to request no flowers, or doubtless there would have been a traffic jam of florist's vans too. It wasn't that I didn't appreciate people's love and concern—I was very grateful for it—but the sheer scale of the response was simply very difficult for the six of us to deal with. At about 4 pm I went with my sisters Liza and Mauny to Beaconsfield, to register Roy's death; it was the first quiet moment I had had all day.

It may seem odd that our activities were dominated by the press in this way; it didn't occur to any of us to shut the door and tell them to go away and leave us to grieve in private. This was not because we wanted publicity; neither Roy nor I had ever sought publicity, even when Roy was working on the stage and on television. All he ever wanted was to do his job as well as he could. That brought him all the work he needed. But inevitably that work brought him into the public eye, and so we were used to seeing his picture in the newspaper and on TV. The press were almost as much a part of our everyday experience of life as the milkman!

Once his cancer was diagnosed and it became known that he was fighting the disease Roy developed another role, cheering and encouraging his many fellow-sufferers. Many patients and their carers wrote to tell us how much it helped to see Roy facing treatments and the side-effects of treatment (such as his baldness) with such courage and good humour, and how thrilled they were to receive a postcard or a phone call from him to cheer them on. Only his role as a public figure enabled him to do this—a strange kind of power but a real one in our modern world.

Additionally, once Roy became involved with fund-raising for the Cause for Hope Appeal, he realised that publicity was a lifeline for the fund. That was the reason for the endless photo-calls and interviews and the tremen-

dous Tour of Hope which visited so many cities. The aim
was to touch as many people's lives as possible, to raise
everyone's awareness of the disease and the need for
research to beat it, and to collect the much-needed
money to fund the Centre. We knew that the press were
invaluable allies in enabling this to happen.

Finally, although we never tried to manipulate situations, we were always honest with anyone who interviewed us about our Christian faith and our allegiance
to the Lord Jesus Christ. We never grabbed anyone by the
collar and asked them if they were saved! But we always
took every opportunity to show that we were ordinary
Christians, doing our best to follow Jesus, and living out
our lives in the way we believed he wanted us to.

This was why when Roy died I carried on just as we
had always lived, accepting the role of the press as part of
our life, and giving interviews and photographs as a kind
of due, a repayment to the public for all the support and
affection they had shown our family over the years and
especially during the last few months of Roy's illness.

In fact I had scarcely had time to analyse my own feelings
on that first day when Roy died. I had been busy all day,
and I had to remain calm to give interviews and to allow
the TV crews the shots they wanted for filming, walking
down the garden and holding photos of Roy. My overwhelming sensation was one of relief that Roy was no
longer in pain. Because we had been prepared for his
death for so long, it did not come as so much of a shock.
Grief was not a new experience into which I had been
thrust suddenly, because I think I had been grieving for
him for a long time already.

I was very tired, though, and I didn't feel at all hungry.

Julia kept following me round the house with tasty morsels, trying to tempt me to eat something, but all I could manage were little pieces of bread, and hot milk and honey. Julia was worried, too, that I wouldn't be able to sleep, and even went to the chemist and asked for a mild sleeping pill to help me. In fact I was exhausted and slept deeply that night when the house was finally quiet. The sleeping tablet was redundant, and remained that way.

The next day Jim Graham, our pastor, came back from Ireland where he had been attending a conference, and came to see us. I asked him if I could speak at a service at church one Sunday, to thank everyone for all their prayers for Roy. He said, 'Yes, whenever you're ready.' I replied, 'I'm ready now,' so we arranged it for the next day. I knew that many of our friends had gone on praying for Roy's healing, long after all hope—in earthly terms—had gone. I wanted to thank them for that, but I didn't want them to be bewildered by Roy's dying. I wanted them all to know that Roy had died on God's appointed day.

On Sunday I walked to church early to pray with Jim and to sort out some arrangements, only to find, to my horror, a camera team from Carlton Television waiting. I nearly changed my mind about the whole thing. I was very much afraid that people might think that by offering to stand up and speak in church I was pushing myself into the limelight, and that it had been set up. In the end I went through with it. After all, I reasoned, if it was the right thing to do without the press there, it was no less right just because they had turned up unexpectedly. I really couldn't keep worrying about what people might think. It was harder to talk to all our friends at church with the cameras there, but I managed it, and thanked them for all their love and support.

In many ways the constant attention of the press was a help—it kept me focused on what was important. All the interviews asked basic questions about how Roy would be remembered, how he had faced death, and how I was coping with bereavement. Over and over again I was able to tell people of the great Christian expectation, and that Roy had not feared death because he knew where he was going, to be with the Lord Jesus. Although he had grown weary of the pain and suffering on the path to death, he had never lost his sense of humour, and even in the last days he was smiling and saying 'Happy Birthday' to himself. I was secure in knowing that he was now free of pain, and I trusted Jesus to look after him for me, so although I missed him dreadfully, I could only rejoice in his release from his body.

One major job in those first days was dealing with the mail. We received at least one sack each day for the first week, and we hardly had time even to open all those envelopes. However, I was determined that every letter should have a reply of some sort, and a student friend came in to help. We divided them into three piles. Those from total strangers received a formal note thanking them for their messages; those from people who had written a more personal letter received a typed letter to which I added a handwritten postscript; and I wrote personal letters to all our friends. Just addressing all the envelopes was a major burden on top of all the other activities, but it was wonderful to hear from so many people who had cared about Roy over many years, and I was so grateful for such love and support.

The most urgent task was to make plans for the thanksgiving service, and I was determined to make time to do that properly. I gathered the family together, and we put

'Do not disturb' signs on the front and back doors and took the phone off the hook! I was not sure quite how we would manage, but we prayed together for guidance, and then we each offered our ideas. I wanted a simple, home-spun service, which would honour God and pay tribute to Roy, for all the local people, the neighbours and shop-keepers who had known him for years. It all fell into place with great harmony, and when Jim arrived to join the discussion he accepted all our suggestions happily. One fear was that the church would be under siege from the press and people wanting to watch, and our quiet funeral for family and church friends would become a spectacle. Whenever I had spoken to friends who lived a long way away I had put them off coming to the service, by promis-ing that we would hold a public memorial service in London in the near future, somewhere that would hold a large number of people, and more easily accessible than Gerrards Cross.

After I had given that first interview to Sky TV on Friday morning after Roy died, they had asked if I would let them film the service. I really didn't want anything to intrude on the service, and I certainly didn't want it to turn into a production, but I said that if the church office agreed, they could put in one camera. In fact it quickly became clear that allowing Sky to film would be a help: there would be only one camera team in church (and they promised to be unobtrusive), and they would allow the rest of the television news services to pick up the pictures from their base in Croydon. They also helped by setting up sound systems and closed-circuit TV screens in the church hall and outside the church, so that all the over-spill crowds could still take part.

Harry Secombe was away on holiday. I rang him in

Majorca to tell him what was planned, but I told him not to worry about coming home. 'It's all right,' he replied. 'Myra's had our bags packed since last Wednesday!' The funeral would be on the afternoon of Thursday, 8th September; it was Harry's birthday.

Roy's body was cremated in the morning, at a separate event at the crematorium. We didn't tell anyone that there would be no coffin at the service in church, because we wanted the morning to be completely private for the immediate family. We worked very hard at this, arranging for the hearse to come to the crematorium alone, and making our own way there separately in our own cars, so there was no 'procession' to follow. This was our 'time to weep'. Fortunately this time the press did not find out what was happening; two reporters did turn up, but we asked them to leave and they did so—though I confess I kept looking towards the bushes to make sure no more were lurking anywhere! The service at the crematorium was short and simple, led lovingly by our own pastor, Jim Graham. The only decoration was a large spray of autumn flowers and leaves in golds and browns, which looked like a warm splash of golden sunshine.

I think it was the bleakest moment of my life when I watched the hearse come up the drive to the crematorium. We were all gathered in the ante-room, and as I looked out of the window at the coffin being lifted, the subdued chatter of the others made me want to scream, 'Can't you all be quiet? That's my husband in there.' Any kind of conversation was intolerable to me just then. Julia cried and Anne Graham comforted her, but I didn't dare cry. I knew that if I let go then I would be unable to stop.

Roy's ashes were scattered. I didn't want them put in a

special place or on to a special flower bed; once his spirit had gone, his body was not important to me, because it wasn't him any more. I can understand that some people wish to cherish even those remains, and this is part of their way of working through their grief. A good friend of mine, for instance, scattered the ashes of her husband in places they loved, where they had been happy together. Some people keep the ashes in a jar on the shelf! I simply didn't feel the need for this and decided that it wasn't worth making a fuss about it.

After the cremation we went home for lunch; more friends had arrived for the afternoon funeral service— Cliff Richard, Joan Morecambe (Eric's widow) and her daughter Gail and granddaughter Amelia (who is my god-daughter), Rob Parsons and others. We had arranged a simple ploughman's lunch, but even that is complicated to serve to thirty-five people. In the middle of it all, as we were rushing around, Julia said in exasperation, 'Oh, where's Dad?!' I knew what she meant—he was always good at jollying things along, and we could just have done with his help!

Harry Secombe was very emotional. As it was his birthday I had bought him a silly present, a sort of toy duck, and he didn't know whether to laugh or cry. A funeral lunch party is incredibly difficult to host, as people are afraid to be happy.

At the church there were crowds of people, and it was difficult to see and greet everyone. A TV screen had been placed outside the church for those who couldn't get inside; it was a blustery day with the odd shower, but still a crowd stood there throughout the service. I don't think anyone got too wet.

The day before we had received a most inspired gift

from a friend, the manager of a nearby hotel where Roy and I sometimes swam. It was a huge bouquet of helium balloons covered with clowns and stars. We took them to the church and placed them at one side, where they bobbed and floated: an ideal remembrance of Roy's impish humour. On the other side was a large blown-up picture of Roy.

Daniel, Anto and Ben played in the church orchestra, and Julia read from Psalm 112. Harry Secombe spoke about Roy the entertainer: 'He was the best of us . . . he had more talent than the rest of us . . . he could sing, he could dance, he could act, he could write, he could play lots of instruments—and if he'd taken up embroidery, he'd have been a record-breaker at that, too!' Rob Parsons spoke about Roy the family man, and the joy he found in our marriage and in the four children. Daniel spoke of Roy the father, and his wife Birthe read from Exodus 34:6-7: 'The Lord, the Lord, the compassionate and gracious God, slow to anger, abounding in love and faithfulness, maintaining love to thousands, and forgiving wickedness, rebellion and sin.' Ray Donnelly described Roy working tirelessly for the Lung Cancer fund, and told how he had watched Roy visiting a cancer ward and speaking to every patient with a smile and joke and a special word, even though he was at the time very ill himself. Anto read from *Living Light*, and Les Moir spoke about Roy's last music recording session, making a jazz praise album with Benjamin. I told everyone about Roy's birthday, which was the last day he was really conscious. He had suddenly raised both his arms and said, 'Jesus Christ is my Saviour! Jesus Christ is my Lord!—Hey Jesus!' Carl McGregor sang a wonderful song, which spoke so well of the family's feelings, and got the whole congregation dancing:

> He's turned my mourning into dancing again.
> He's lifted my sorrow,
> I can't stay silent,
> I must sing for his joy has come.
>
> Where there once was only hurt
> He gave his healing hand.
> Where there once was only pain
> He brought comfort like a friend.

All in all it was a joyful occasion. We remembered Roy and we laughed and sang his favourite hymns—all good jazzy arrangements!—in the building where he had worshipped for seventeen years.

After the service we went back to the house for a cup of tea. It seemed to be a very long one—after an hour and a half there were still fifty people in the house! At the end of the day, after everyone had gone, Jim Graham came to pray with us, which helped us a great deal. At the funeral he had reminded us of Roy's words: 'The day of my funeral—that will be my finest performance!'

Over the last few months of Roy's illness, we had realised that he was going to die. Mostly I was so busy, just getting through each day, that I didn't have much time to worry about the future or how I would cope after he was dead. After his death there were times—especially at night—when fears would 'crowd around me', but mostly I just kept going. Every day was still so busy, getting things organised and carrying on with those parts of Roy's work which I could do—speaking about the Lung Cancer

Fund, for instance—that I had no time to feel sorry for myself.

Sometimes I was tempted to feel that Roy's death was 'the failure of my plans'. He had not been healed, he had not lived to see the Lung Cancer Centre established, there was no triumph. And then I would always realise that God's purposes were being worked out, not our earthly plans and desires. God had taken Roy to himself in his own time, and Roy had touched many lives before he died.

I wasn't always able to be confident and positive. Two weeks after the funeral I was asked to appear on a new programme about faith, to be broadcast on Sunday mornings. Sue Cook was interviewing me and being very sweet and helpful, but the recording didn't go smoothly. Several parts had to be done two or three times and I began to get muddled. I couldn't remember whether or not I was repeating myself. I felt very inadequate and was sure I was making a mess of it. In addition, it was the first time since Roy had died that I had been to London on my own. Suddenly just the effort of getting myself around seemed exhausting and threatening, and I felt very vulnerable.

I realise now that it was very soon after Roy's death, and I was still reeling from all the events of the previous six months. I knew that I was capable of carrying on and running my own life, but I felt raw and bruised and tearful. It was a very low moment.

One of the hardest things to deal with is being told by other people how I should be feeling. Of course I have had some bad times, but according to some people, I don't have nearly enough of them! Many otherwise kind people seem to take a pleasure in being directive about responses to grief: 'You will be feeling dreadful,' they say, and seem to sit back and watch for it. At Christmas we had so many deeply gloomy cards predicting our misery ('We know how sad you will be at Christmas . . . you will miss Roy more than ever') that it became a family joke. As we opened our presents or started carving the turkey Ben would ask, 'Are we having a terrible time yet?' In fact we had a lovely Christmas, just as Roy would have wanted us to. We laughed a lot and cried a little, and remembered him all the time with love and joy.

In fact it isn't necessarily the anniversaries or special days which are difficult, but little things: finding a letter, seeing an item of clothing, catching sight of someone in a crowded street who walks the same way as Roy . . .

Mostly I just get on with life, just like everyone else. The difficulty is that if I am normal and happy, people suggest that I have not yet come through to reality, and that sooner or later I will crack up and succumb to grief. I am perfectly willing to accept that this may be the case—I don't pretend to know everything that will happen—but it doesn't seem to have happened yet. I know that Roy is with Jesus and that gives me great peace. I am greatly blessed by a loving family and friends, and I know that as I commit every day to the Lord, I am walking in his will. I am sorry if my joy offends anyone, but I cannot be less than honest about who I am and what I feel, because I can only ever be honest with God, the Father who knows all our hearts. 'The dreams of all I hope to be, the truth of what I am.' After all, that is why Jesus came, to release us from all our posturing and pretences into his glorious love and light, to be truly ourselves.

CHAPTER FOUR

Sunshine and Shadow

For the tears that flow in secret
In the broken times;
For the moments of elation,
Or the troubled mind—

I have never been a great weeper. This is partly because I was brought up to be 'sensible'; our wartime generation was taught that it was admirable to be brave and to endure. The boarding school I attended disapproved of any display of emotion, so I quickly learned to suppress my feelings. I could weep easily on stage or when I was watching films, but I hardly ever cried during my own personal crises. However, tears can be very therapeutic, and I have certainly discovered the release of crying over the past few years.

When Roy was first diagnosed as having lung cancer, the shock brought tears with it for the first twenty-four hours or so, while my mind and emotions adjusted to the possibilities ahead of us. It was when we told Ben about Roy, and I watched him struggling to keep his composure, that I realised how important it was that we should be free to express how we were feeling. So often we repress our tears in order not to embarrass other people, but within the family we had to be able to be ourselves, to support one another and to give each other permission to be sad.

Outside the family, though, I understand how awkward it makes people feel to see others crying; friends feel helpless in the face of the open expression of grief which they cannot cure. So I developed a way of 'diverting' my tears at inopportune times, and determinedly thinking about something else to drive the tears away. After a few weeks I realised that I was getting headaches, and occasionally taking aspirin to relieve them—something I usually try not to do. I soon realised that all I needed to do was to allow the tears to flow, and then the headaches disappeared. Crying was a way of releasing the stress of pent-up emotions, and had a healing and calming effect.

For many years Roy worked on the *Record Breakers* programme on Children's BBC, presenting other people's record-breaking attempts and achieving quite a few himself. After his death, the next series started by devoting the first programme to all Roy's records, as a tribute to him. It showed clips of all his daring exploits over the years: parascending under the bridges on the Thames, wing-walking on a plane flying to France across the channel, and tap-dancing his way into the record books. It was a very moving tribute, and I sat and watched it on TV with Julia and Benj. Cheryl Baker had been Roy's colleague and co-presenter on the programme, and as the last clip ended she was supposed to turn professionally to the camera and speak the lines from the script. Instead, with tears pouring down her face, she said, 'I'm sorry, Roy,' and put her head in her hands. Just as we were watching this the phone rang. We all looked at each other and said together, 'I can't answer it,' because we were all crying. When I did blow my nose and answer the phone, it was a friend who had been watching the show and who was also in floods of tears.

Nowadays the tears come to me much more easily. One occasion when I found it very hard to control my feelings was when I was being photographed for the Appeal Fund in a room full of huge photos of Roy. While the others were busy setting up the cameras I looked around at all the pictures of my husband, and on an impulse I privately kissed the tip of my finger and touched it to his face. In an instant my eyes filled up with tears and I had to smother myself in a large tissue very quickly. I'm sure the photos they took of me must have been rather pink and blotchy ones!

I still try hard not to become emotional in public, though; I try to be aware of other people's feelings, and I know that often they are scared about how I'll react if they talk about Roy. The tone was set by that first Sky interview, when Alison, the interviewer, was obviously nervous about having to approach me a few hours after Roy's death. I was so keen to reassure her that I decided I had to be very normal and relaxed.

The same approach worked well when I went to the local shops. I went with a smile and talked to people, and then they didn't feel they had to avoid me. Often people who have been bereaved are made to feel even more isolated because friends who don't know what to say dare not telephone or visit them. I jump right in and chat to people, so their difficulty disappears. The morning after Roy's funeral service I went to Pop-In, the mums' and toddlers' group organised by our church, to make the tea and coffee as usual; otherwise the mums and the other helpers might have been wondering how I was going to react. I went in and spoke about Roy and behaved as normally as possible. I thought it was best to get on with life straight away, and let them see that life goes on.

These experiences have affected me in other ways, too. I think that I have become much more sensitive to other people's grief, because I have been through it myself. In the summer of 1995 I watched the celebrations in memory of VE Day alone at home. I found myself thinking of all the wives and mothers fifty years ago, who had seen their husbands and sons go off to war. I thought of all the life, talent and potential of those young men, and how they must have felt at the possibility of losing all that. I found myself weeping for the pain of all those women, and weeping over humanity's behaviour. It seemed to me then that mankind will never learn the lessons of war, because there is always a new generation growing up which has not experienced it at first hand. So we see the rise of the National Front and the Neo-Nazi groups among young people in Europe, even as their grandparents are remembering the war they fought to defeat such ideologies. It was all the more poignant because the national grief and mourning were mixed with a strong sense of repentance for all that happened in those war years, on all sides.

Bereavement seems to open up the emotions. All deaths seem more immediate, more vivid to me now, because I have seen it so close at hand, and I feel I can more truly share in the sorrow of other people.

At the same time I know that all deaths are part of the great cycle of life: the leaves fall to feed the soil, the seeds die to germinate again, and our earthly bodies die while our spirits go on to heavenly life. If we stand on God's side of it we know there is an eternal pattern and purpose to everything that happens, and this can help us to endure our own pain. But that intellectual knowledge, though it helps us to understand and explain, does not enable us to stand outside our own emotions, and it does not allow us to escape from or deny the pain of our loss.

There is no way out of grief but through it. There is no magic formula, no spiritual or emotional trick which can let us off the hook. The passage of time may eventually

57

enable us to get used to the feeling of being alone, but not even that will change the fact of our bereavement. The Holy Spirit will bring us comfort and peace, but God will not protect us from the reality of what it is to be human. He wants our eyes to be open to that reality, and fixed upon Jesus. He knew the greatest pain it is possible for mankind to know—injustice, desolation, desertion and a cruel and painful death. He knows and shares our grief, and he shows us how to face it: not with bitterness or anger, but with love and gentleness. If we fix our eyes upon him, we can find a way through our distress.

We cannot escape from grief, but we can choose how we go through it. We can allow ourselves to be defeated by grief, or we can survive it. I am not suggesting a false cheerfulness which only puts a mask over our feelings— that would be dishonest to ourselves and to everyone else. But we can apply the considerable power of our will to decide how we will approach this experience. We can decide whether we will collapse before the cold wind of grief, or whether we will bend in the wind like a young tree, and spring back to grow up towards the sun. As everything we do and everything we see reminds us of our loved one, we can choose either to be swamped with sorrow at every turn, or we can rejoice in the happy memories which come flooding back.

Several people warned me about how difficult it would be to clear out Roy's clothes—but does it have to be? I tried to tackle the job cheerfully; after all, if Roy had been there and decided that he didn't need them, he would gladly have given them away. One day, though, I found a pair of his trousers which had escaped my clearing out, because they were in the washing basket. I washed and ironed them and carried them upstairs to the wardrobe, and then suddenly burst into tears. It hit me all over again that I wouldn't be washing things or caring for him any more.

When Roy worked in cabaret, he was often asked to do special shows for companies. He had a long song with the chorus 'Tooralai, tooralai, tooralai-ay', to which he would make up extra verses. He would get someone in the firm to tell him details of all the well-known characters, the managers, secretaries, directors and foremen, and then he would put on glasses, false teeth or a wig, and imitate them. It always got a tremendous response—but it required an extensive wardrobe of props.

Now Roy was a hoarder: he kept everything, and he often bought items—a funny hat, a scarf or a wig—when he saw them, 'just in case' they ever came in useful. But when the time came he could never find the item he wanted, and would invariably have to go out and buy another. After he died I started to clear out the room behind the garage which he used for rehearsing, and found the most enormous quantity of boxes and bags, full of props, pins, sewing things, hats and so on. It could have been deeply depressing, and I could have mourned over every item he had chosen and used. Instead, as Antonia said, 'Guess who's got the last laugh?' I had always complained about the amount of stuff Roy hoarded, and now I was the one having to clear it all out. I had to give in and laugh with him!

This important matter of being honest with myself includes being honest about Roy. People often put him on a pedestal because he was well known and because of his bravery and selflessness during his illness. That is all true, and I admire and love him for that. But at the same time he was an ordinary bloke, he wasn't perfect and neither am I, and sometimes he irritated me! This is part of choosing how to face bereavement: I am sad and I miss Roy, but I still view him clearly, as the real person he was.

I don't want him to be canonised by death, because I don't want his memory to be changed from the person I knew. If I were to pretend that he was other than he was, if I were to fantasise and let him become some kind of perfect person in my mind just because he is dead, I would lose him even more thoroughly than I have lost him now. I need the real memories of our real life together, warts and all, to sustain me—not some fairy-tale. Being honest about those things somehow makes them more bearable.

Another aspect of dealing with the sorrow of these 'broken times' is learning how to distinguish between genuine grief and self-pity. There are so many moments, especially in the early days after a death, when grief threatens to overwhelm us. One of the most common for me was the mistaken recognitions—when I would catch sight of someone in a crowd whose back view looked just like Roy's, or who walked in the same way, and my mind, caught unawares, would think, 'There's Roy!' The mistake was only momentary, and then realisation would flood in, but the pain would be intense. This is a natural part of grieving, as the unconscious mind learns to catch up with what the conscious mind knows, and we must allow ourselves to experience this sorrow.

One day, however, I was returning from Scotland, and arrived at Heathrow during a busy rush hour. Lots of people were standing around waiting to meet arrivals, and my eye was caught by a pretty young girl who was anxiously searching the sea of faces in the hall. Then a man approached her, recognition and delight spread across her face, and she threw herself into his arms. I found myself bursting into uncontrollable tears. There was no one to meet me. I had lost that special relationship for ever, and I felt more cold and alone in that moment than I had for a long time.

Then I realised that I was envious of the young couple and their love; love which Roy and I had experienced in our time. I was simply wallowing in self-pity—poor old me, I used to have someone like that, but not any more. It was too much like watching an old movie on television—I could almost hear the orchestra!—and I gave myself a stern talking-to. Grief is natural, and a process we must undergo, but self-pity is unattractive and self-centred. It is important to distinguish between the two.

I think that discerning this difference early on was very helpful to me. I learned to let go with real grief, but to control any impulses towards self-pity. Self-pity tends towards envy of what others may be enjoying, and it centres on some obscure sense that we have been deprived of something to which we have a right. Whenever I begin to feel like this I remind myself that I have no rights, because my life is not my own. I gave my life to Christ—and I didn't add a postscript, 'And please make it a wonderful life, and protect me from all pain.'

There were some very bleak times during the last part of Roy's life when we both felt that God had abandoned us; we felt no comfort, and no respite from the onslaught. I started to question the reality of my faith and what would happen if I abandoned God. That in itself brought comfort as I realised that there was nowhere else to go, no one in the world I could completely trust. I reminded myself of the transformation Jesus had made in the whole of my life when I discovered this spiritual reality. From there I began to 'enter into his suffering' by knowing a little of what Jesus himself must have felt when he was separated from God on the cross by my sin. Jesus who was sinless cried out to his Father, 'My God, my God, why have you forsaken me?' because sin came between him and God. Jesus was alone then, so what right had I to complain?

Some time ago I came across this beautiful but anonymous meditation.

He had no rights:
No right to a soft bed, and a well-laid table;
No right to a home of his own, a place where his own pleasure might be sought;
No right to choose pleasant, congenial companions, those who could understand him and sympathise with him;
No right to shrink away from contact with sin, to pull his garments closer around him and walk in cleaner paths;
No right to be understood and appreciated; no not by those on whom he had poured out a double portion of his love;
No right even never to be forsaken by his Father, the one who meant more than all to him.

His only right was to endure shame, spitting, blows; to take his place as a sinner at the dock; to bear my sins in anguish on the cross.
He had no rights. And I?
A right to the comforts of life? No, but a right to the love of God for my pillow.
A right to physical safety? No, but a right to the security of being in his will.
A right to love and sympathy from those around me? No, but a right to the friendship of the one who understands me better than I do myself.

A right to be a leader among men? No, but a right to be led
by the one to whom I have given my all, led as a little child,
with its hand in the hand of its father.

A right to a home, and dear ones? No, not necessarily; but a
right to dwell in the heart of God.

A right to myself? No, but oh, I have a right to Christ.

All that he takes I will give;
All that he gives I will take;
He, my only right! He, the one right before which all other
rights fade into nothingness.
I have full right to him: Oh, may he have full right to me!

Now when I have any doubts or fears, envy or self-pity, I
go back to Psalm 139:

Where can I go from your Spirit?
Where can I flee from your presence?
If I go up to the heavens, you are there;
If I make my bed in the depths, you are there. If I rise on the
wings of the dawn,
if I settle on the far side of the sea,
even there your hand will guide me,
your right hand will hold me fast.

If I say, 'Surely the darkness will hide me
and the light become night around me,'
even the darkness will not be dark to you;
the night will shine like the day
for darkness is as light to you (Psalm 139:7–12).

It reminds me where my real security lies. Who else am I
to turn to? I have nothing else to do in my life but follow
the Lord. When we follow Jesus we put away all thoughts
of rights or personal desires, and fix our eyes only on
serving him in his will. Self-pity has no place in a life of
service.

Real grief, however, I have to deal with in my own way. If I am busy, I may have to bottle up my emotions for a while—it is my concern and I don't have to inflict it on everyone else—but when I am alone I let go and have a good cry. It's positive, healthy and therapeutic, and I always feel better afterwards. I find it easiest to cry in my prayer-time, when I am talking to the Lord about Roy, or about the things I can't do without him. Sometimes I say to Jesus, 'I am missing him dreadfully—please give him a hug from me.' It's wonderful to have a Father who knows all our feelings and thoughts, so we can be completely honest about them.

> O Lord, you have searched me and you know me.
> You know when I sit and when I rise;
> you perceive my thoughts from afar.
> You discern my going out and my lying down;
> you are familiar with all my ways.
> Before a word is on my tongue
> you know it, Lord (Psalm 39:1–4).

One reason for my determined rejection of anything which smacks of self-pity is that I have indulged in it too much in the past. Long ago when the children were small I suffered periodic bouts of depression. Although I know that often there is nothing we can do about real clinical depression, nevertheless sometimes I wallowed in it; now I am very wary of anything which allows me to think too much about 'poor old me'.

I try very hard not to be an object of pity. Sympathy is very welcome and a comfort, but pity has a corrosive effect on our will. We are very easily convinced that our situation is so awful that no effort from us can make it any better. And of course, being in that condition can be very comfortable, in a painful sort of way. After all, if things are really that bad, no one can expect us to do anything; we are relieved of all responsibility.

I am reminded of Jesus' words to the man at the pool of Bethesda: 'Do you want to get well?'

Now there is in Jerusalem near the Sheep Gate a pool, which in Aramaic is called Bethesda, and which is surrounded by five covered colonnades. Here a great number of disabled people used to lie—the blind, the lame, the paralysed. One who was there had been an invalid for thirty-eight years. When Jesus saw him lying there and learned that he had been in that condition for a long time, he asked him, 'Do you want to get well?'

'Sir,' the invalid replied, 'I have no one to help me into the pool when the water is stirred. While I am trying to get in, someone else goes down ahead of me.'

Then Jesus said to him, 'Get up! Pick up your mat and walk.' At once the man was cured; he picked up his mat and walked (John 5:2–9a).

The story of the pool of Bethesda was that from time to time an angel would come down and stir up the waters, and whoever was first into the pool after such a disturbance would be cured of whatever disease he had. In thirty-eight years the man had never managed to be the lucky one.

Jesus' question would seem to be a foolish one. The man was an invalid—why ask him whether he wanted to be cured? Of course he did; anyone would want to be cured. I wonder how deeply Jesus saw into that man's soul. After all that time, he knew no other life than that of an invalid. Indeed, in Israel in those days, with no Welfare State to provide for him, the man was probably a beggar, and doubtless knew of no other way of making a living. A

65

beggar with an obvious disability would be a more likely candidate for receiving charity from kindly passers-by; if the man was healed, he might well lose some of his income!

I think that often, when we are in the depths of despair at our circumstances, and asking Jesus for help, he responds by asking us the same question: 'Do you want to be well?' Do we really want our circumstances to change, or have we become so accustomed to them that change would feel risky and unsafe? Are we willing to throw the crutch away and go unnoticed in the crowd? Or have we begun to enjoy the attention it gets us, the allowances that are made for us?

It is these ideas which have made me so wary of self-pity. I am determined not to make excuses for myself, and not to let other people make them for me. That way I avoid the temptation to become lazy, or self-centred or self-indulgent. That was why, for a while after Roy's funeral, I refused to wear black, in case it appeared that I was making a production out of mourning!

Even the worst of grief, however, is not entirely black. The first glimpses of these 'moments of elation' came on the Sunday evening after Roy died. I was at a Communion service at church, praising God because we are told to 'praise him in everything' and that 'God inhabits the praises of his people'. I was thinking about Roy at the same time. Suddenly I saw a picture in my mind, of Roy and Jesus in a boat together, grinning and waving across the waves at me! I was praising Jesus and smiling at the same time, because it made me so happy to realise that Roy was united with his Lord. I thought, 'That's it! If I praise God with all my heart I will see Roy with Jesus and that will bring me comfort.' The next Sunday I was in church again, and I thought how wonderful it would be to experience that same feeling of reassurance and joy, knowing that Roy was safe and happy with Jesus. So I tried to recapture that picture, by praising Jesus in the same way as before. But this time the picture I saw was different: I seemed to see Roy and Jesus together, but turning their backs on me and walking away to something new. I realised that God never lets us stand still, and that already I had to be prepared to let Roy go, in my mind, into his new life. Nevertheless these pictures were a great source of comfort to me.

Another comfort was a verse from the Bible which leapt out at me with new meaning: 'Therefore, since we are surrounded with such a great cloud of witnesses, let us throw off everything that hinders and the sin that so easily entangles, and let us run with perseverance the race marked out for us' (Hebrews 12:1). I felt very strongly that this was a word meant for me at this time, all the more because my niece and several others also came across the same words and felt that they should pass them on to me.

Ever since then I have sensed Roy watching this life on earth, from the grandstand, as it were, with all the saints—the great cloud of witnesses—cheering us on. At the same time I can look up to Roy and all the other Christians who have passed this way before me, and know that I am not alone in facing difficulties. They have run the race of faith before us and have made it by faith. Sometimes it fills me with longing to be able to talk to Roy, because he now sees Jesus face to face, and he knows the answers to many of my questions. Am I walking in the perfect will of God? What would he want me to do in certain situations? Sometimes I wish I could just phone him and ask him!

There is yet another side to self-awareness about grief: not only do I have to give myself permission to grieve, to weep when my tears are genuine grief and not self-pity, but I also have to give myself permission to be happy.

Of course I am sad that Roy has died, and I miss him all the time. Yet there are still moments of fun; we have always been a family that laughs a lot, and that hasn't changed. The children and I share many jokes; my heart lifts up when I praise Jesus and share in worship with other Christians; and on a day-to-day basis I am very contented. None of this means that I love and miss Roy any less.

There is a great temptation to feel guilty about being happy. 'I have just lost my husband—how can I possibly be happy?' It is almost as if grieving is a way of staying close to the loved one, and that to stop grieving—even for a minute—is disloyal, a suggestion that the loss doesn't matter. It isn't true, of course; quite the opposite. I know that Roy wants me to be happy, because he always wanted my life to be as good as possible; he always wanted the best for me. It was part of his love for me, and my love for him isn't changed in any way as I get on with the rest of my life.

Once again I have to exercise my will—my ability to choose how I will go through my grief. I will not wallow in self-pity, but I will allow myself to grieve honestly. I will not cling to sadness and depression, but I will allow myself to rejoice and give thanks for happiness and contentment, for 'the moments of elation'—because they also are a gift from God.

A favourite photo,
taken by Antonia.

A gala concert at Liverpool Empire in aid of Cause for Hope.
Who's your friend?

Arriving at Lime Street Station, Liverpool
at the start of the Tour of Hope.

Arriving at Waterloo, seeing the crowds waiting to greet Roy.

Roy has an engine named after him.

Arriving at Waterloo at the end of the Tour of Hope.

The second Tour of Hope – Pulled by Roy's engine.

Receiving the Freedom of the City of Liverpool.

*Receiving an award on behalf of ASH from
HRH the Duke of Gloucester.*

*After the foundation
stone laying ceremony
(for the building of the
research centre) 29
May 1996, beside a
huge mural of Roy.*

CHAPTER FIVE

Praying in God's Will

For all the disappointments
Or the sting of old regrets;
All my prayers and longings
That seem unanswered yet—

I suppose my greatest disappointment ever was that Roy was not completely healed from his cancer. At the end of his first course of treatment he seemed so well that I felt sure the final check-up would confirm his health. How we would rejoice when we told the world that he was healed! But when the results came back, they were inconclusive. Roy was very well, the tumour had disappeared off the X-ray completely, but a bronchoscopy revealed that there were still cancer cells in the lung. They might be dead, they might lie dormant, or they might start multiplying again. No one could say for sure how long Roy would remain well.

It was a bitter moment for me. I had been so sure that our prayers would be answered. Hadn't the Lord told me, right at the beginning of his illness, 'Stand back and see what I will do'? I had been so sure that God's plan for Roy would include his healing. After all we had been through, after all Roy had suffered through the early treatment, surely we deserved healing? That was when I realised how flawed and human my thinking was. Deep down, I was still thinking that we could deserve some-thing—yet I knew that when we become Christians, we give up all rights to our own lives.

I had to repent of that kind of thinking. Long ago we had put our lives into God's hands, and had agreed to trust him for everything. Paul urges us 'to offer your bodies as living sacrifices, holy and pleasing to God—

this is your spiritual act of worship' (Romans 12:1). We often pray, 'Lord, make my life a living sacrifice.' Then, when the Lord takes us at our word, we start whining. The fact is that we all hope that God's will for us entails no difficulties or dangers, no struggles for the body or the will. Yet how else is God to teach us the lessons of faithfulness and trust and love which he wants his children to learn?

It was through that great disappointment that I realised how much I still had to learn—lessons I knew in my head but not in my heart. When we give our lives to God we have to let go of our own desires and wills. I have worked this through for myself, often without realising it, in all the ups and downs of family life. All the time I was pressing for what I wanted, I was constantly frustrated by my inability to make the world revolve around my wants. But whenever I managed to put God first in my life, to say, 'All right, Lord, whatever you want'—then things began to work. Then I was able to experience the peace that comes from placing all our desires at the foot of the cross.

Right from the start Roy had been able to say, 'Well, this isn't the way I would have chosen, Lord, but it's your will, not mine—and if this is your will then it's OK by me.' That willingness to trust God takes the edge off all disappointments, fears and anxieties. Once I learned it life became easier. Then if God closed a door, I was able to accept it and wait for the next opportunity with patience, willing to see what God wanted me to do next.

As the family absorbed the news that Roy's cancer might come back, we committed ourselves afresh to Jesus, and to trusting him in everything. Certainly the time we had with

Roy before he died was very precious, because we knew that it might be short. We made the most of every day. As Roy said once, 'I don't complain any more about standing on a station platform in the rain, because I'm glad to be alive to get wet!' Many years ago we read a very funny book by Bill Cosby, in which he described his elderly parents going for a walk together, stopping for a rest on a bench, and his father taking off his hat and accidentally sitting on it. It became a private joke. Roy would say 'When I sit on my hat . . .' meaning when he was very elderly and absent-minded. He always wanted us to enjoy old age together.

One of the things I am very grateful for is that I had the privilege of two and a half years with Roy after his cancer was first diagnosed. In that time I was able to say to him everything I needed to say, and to tell him how grateful I was to him for being such a good and faithful husband and father. I do not suffer from 'the sting of old regrets' in the sense of feeling that we had any unfinished business between us. It must be very hard for those whose loved ones die suddenly and without warning, because so much is left unsaid.

Far worse must be those situations where the relationship has been difficult. If Roy's cancer had been diagnosed before I became a Christian, I am sure the trauma would have been much greater, because I would have felt so guilty. I have told the story in an earlier book, *Give Us This Day*, of how our marriage began to fail when our children were small and I was suffering from depression. Then a friend showed me how to commit my life to Jesus, and I experienced the peace and love of God. I began to see how to alter my priorities and to try to live in the way God wanted me to. Very quickly, that affected all my other relationships, especially my marriage. I became more relaxed, less neurotic about discipline and neatness, and generally easier to live with! Roy had always been very patient with me, but I hadn't made it easy for him; when I became depressed I also became rather withdrawn, and tended to shut him out. Now I was able to tell him if I was tired or fed up, and we could talk about it. In fact, we got better at talking about everything, and our marriage was much stronger as a result.

Our relationship wasn't perfect, of course, and we had our ups and downs and all the day-to-day irritations of any family. Roy's father used to laugh when he heard people say, 'We've been married fifty years and we've never had a cross word.' He would say, in his inimitable Yorkshire accent, 'If there's never an argument, somebody's the underdog!' Roy and I learned from our disagreements, though. We learned 'not to let the sun go down on our anger', and how to talk things through, so that we never left resentments to fester or little problems to grow. Most of all, we shared our faith in Jesus, so that our marriage had a common aim: to live in God's will. We were very happy together. That was why, when we knew that Roy was dying, there was no need to express anything except sadness. There were no old wounds to heal, nothing to apologise for, no harsh words to wish unsaid.

It is yet another example of the importance of living in God's will every day, because we never know what is around the corner. None of us knows what lies ahead, so we have to take to heart the advice of the old farmer: to 'farm as if you are going to live for ever, and live as though you are going to die tomorrow'.

At Spring Harvest Steve Chalke told a story about Roy

which illustrated this. At Pentecost 1994 there was a nationwide Christian campaign called 'On Fire', and Roy was asked to appear at Central Hall, Westminster, as part of the 'On Fire for London' events. He insisted on going, although he was very ill at the time, and in fact during the main part of the meeting he fainted backstage. Afterwards, however, he was well enough to attend the press conference, and one of the reporters asked him how it felt, knowing that he had only three months to live.

'Knowing that I have three months to live would make me the most privileged person in this room,' he replied. 'Why's that?' responded the reporter. ''Cos you don't know if you've got tomorrow!' Roy knew that no one can really plan for the future; he knew the verses in the Bible that tell us so:

> Now listen, you who say, 'Today or tomorrow we will go to this or that city, spend a year there, carry on business and make money.' Why, you do not even know what will happen tomorrow. What is your life? You are a mist that appears for a little while and then vanishes. Instead, you ought to say, 'If it is the Lord's will, we will live and do this or that.' As it is, you boast and brag (James 4:13–16).

I believe that it was the power of the Holy Spirit which enabled Roy to face all his suffering without bitterness or regrets. When his lung cancer was diagnosed, he realised that it was the kind of cancer which is usually found in heavy smokers—yet he himself had never smoked a cigarette in his life. However, he had worked for many years in smoky nightclubs, inhaling deeply when he played the trumpet, sang or danced. 'Passive smoking'—inhaling the smoke from other people's cigarettes—was the only explanation his doctors could offer.

As a result of this, he not only campaigned tirelessly to raise funds for research into lung cancer, but also spoke out about the dangers of smoking and passive smoking. One of the few times Roy became really angry was when he heard that Baroness Thatcher had signed a very lucrative contract with Philip Morris, the tobacco magnates. He was aware of the tactics being used by tobacco companies to attract sales in developing countries, and he was deeply saddened by the knowledge—first-hand knowledge—of the suffering that would eventually be caused by encouraging addiction to cigarettes. He was due to appear at a reception given by the Royal Association for Disability and Rehabilitation, in honour of their 'People of the Year, 1992' awards, and he discovered that Baroness Thatcher was to be the guest of honour. On that occasion he managed to hide himself behind a row of photographers during the introductions, because he simply felt that in all conscience he could not shake her by the hand. He did this with the minimum of fuss, though as usual one alert journalist noticed him and made a story out of his reluctance. Nevertheless, this act of conscience was made not out of personal resentment on his part, but on principle. He never spoke harshly of all the smokers who choose to gamble with their own health. When one of our children said, 'Oh, Dad, why does this have to happen to you?' he replied, 'Why not me? I'm no different from anyone else.'

This gift of the Holy Spirit which preserves us from indulging in bitterness and regrets is very precious. It is part of the promise, 'The Lord your God goes with you; he will never leave you nor forsake you' (Deuteronomy 31:6) and it is this which keeps us safe in the midst of danger.

'Safe' may not mean physical safety, but the security which holds our spirits and keeps us from despair.

Sometimes I liken our relationship with Jesus to an insurance policy, which doesn't prevent burglaries or burst water pipes, but enables us to deal with the consequences! When Roy did his record-breaking wing-walking stunt, standing strapped to the roof of a light aircraft as it flew across the English Channel, the BBC insured him for a million pounds. This was not a good-luck charm to keep him safe, but a precaution to deal with the results of a possible disaster—to pay for the support of an invalid or widow if accident or death resulted. Christians do not lead charmed lives. We are as susceptible as anyone else to accident, difficulty or tragedy. Jesus says that when we follow him he will not keep us safe *from* trouble, but safe *in* trouble; he does not protect his children from misfortune, but whatever the difficulties, he will be with us and uphold us.

This becomes all the more real when we are facing up to death or the fear of death. How can we endure it? That is when we cash in the insurance policy, and all the riches of Jesus' love are placed in our hands, and the power of the Holy Spirit, the Comforter, is at our disposal. 'The peace of God, which transcends all understanding, will guard your hearts and your minds in Christ Jesus' (Philippians 4:7). This seems to me to sum it up: if our hearts and minds remain stable, fixed firmly and secure, then we will not be disturbed by events, however dreadful. And we can only be 'kept' in the knowledge and love of God by his word, as we study to understand it and to work it out daily in our lives.

So if we call upon the power of the Holy Spirit to release us from bitterness and from 'the sting of old regrets', what of the disappointments? How can we understand how these things fit together? What about the 'prayers and longings/that seem unanswered yet'? My greatest prayer and longing was for Roy to be restored to his family in full health, so why wasn't Roy healed?

The most painful answer to this question, and one which has been suggested to me on more than one occasion, is that we didn't have enough faith. Many Christians seem to subscribe to the view that it is always God's will that everyone should be healed, and that miraculous healing is prevented only by our failure to believe. I find this a difficult area, for I have personally known people who have experienced healing, and others who have not. I have always been grateful for the wisdom of a pastor friend whom I consulted about this right at the beginning of Roy's illness. He counselled us: 'Unless you get a clear word from the Lord specifically saying that he will heal in this case through a miracle, you should not depend on it.' While it is certainly true that sometimes people are healed miraculously, I do not think that we can assume that we can predict God's purposes in all cases, just because an outcome seems desirable to our human minds.

Moreover, it is tragic that people who are already suffering should be hurt by other Christians who criticise them for not having enough faith. Certainly both Roy and I had to make a conscious effort to let go of the feelings of hurt and guilt that this sort of suggestion aroused in us. Such feelings are counter-productive—they waste time and precious emotional energy, because even if the accusation were true, there would be little we could do about it! Roy's response was to say, 'Let's not worry about it. God knows my heart better than I do. Sorry, God, if I'm wrong, and if I don't have enough faith. All I can do is trust you.' We were reminded of the man in the Bible who asked Jesus to heal his son. Jesus said to him, 'Everything is possible for him who believes.' Immediately the man replied, 'I do believe; help me overcome my unbelief!' (Mark 9:24).

In any case, I think this criticism that we have insufficient faith is too glib, too simplistic. It treats God as though he were a slot-machine from which you can get anything you order, if you only insert enough faith coins. We know that our God is not mechanical, but a loving Father, and we can know him personally and trust him, even when things are going badly for us. God is sovereign in our circumstances and we can trust him to bring about his will.

It comforted us to know that other, greater Christians than we are had received similar criticism. David Watson, who died of cancer, went through similar problems; Selwyn Hughes wrote movingly in *Every Day with Jesus* about the death of his wife, and those Bible study notes helped me to come to terms with my own situation.

From time to time another similar suggestion is made: that healing cannot take place when there is insufficient prayer. A man whose daughter had cancer wrote to many churches, asking people to pray for her, as though he could achieve his desire simply by collecting enough prayers. Even though I sympathise with his feelings, I cannot go along with this idea, either. Prayer isn't a commodity that you can pile up. In any case, God is never going to say, 'You didn't have enough.' He will heal, if it is his will, in response to one person's prayer.

No one could have had more prayer than Roy. His position as a well-known celebrity meant that thousands of Christians heard of his illness and prayed for him. Even among our own local community, so many people told our pastor, Jim Graham, that they were praying for Roy, that Jim said he could imagine God saying, 'Oh, do you know him as well?' I know we were supported and encouraged by all those prayers, but I am also sure that God isn't influenced by such inequality as how famous someone is! God shares the pain and cares for all his suffering children, no matter how many or how few their friends.

> Are not two sparrows sold for a penny? Yet not one of them will fall to the ground apart from the will of your Father. And even the very hairs of your head are numbered. So don't be afraid; you are worth more than many sparrows (Matthew 10:29).

I do believe that for all of us there is a time to die, and that God's purposes and timing may not be fully understood by us as we operate on our human scale. Many people have said to me how sad it was that Roy should die so young, and that he should die before his time. My response is that he did not die before his time—that those were his allotted days. In the graveyard of Grewelthorpe village church, Yorkshire, there is a memorial to a girl who died at the age of seventeen. It says, 'She asked life of thee, and thou gavest her a long life, even for ever and ever.'

In the case of long-drawn-out illness, we often experience great relief when the pain is over, and God takes the sufferer to be with him. A friend whose little daughter died wrote to say that it would be selfish of us to want our loved ones back, 'because they are experiencing something so wonderful with Jesus'. The problem is always that we view our situation with our human eyes, and the limitations of our human time-scheme. We are grieving for our own loss of expectations. God has greater purposes to fulfil, which often we cannot comprehend.

It is only now, with hindsight, that I can begin to make sense of the fact that Roy was not healed of his cancer. Of course, healing would have been a tremendous witness to the miracle-working power of God (and the wisdom and skills of the doctors who fought the battle against cancer with Roy are also a part of that power). Yet God had other purposes in mind. If Roy had been healed, that would have been wonderful; yet many others daily are not healed—would they have been helped by our victory? Perhaps, but I cannot help thinking that they were helped far more by the fact that Roy trusted God for the outcome and continued to have faith and hope right to the end. A complete cure would have set him apart. Because his case was 'ordinary' like theirs, other sufferers can identify with him. His story can encourage them to understand that with the help of the Holy Spirit, a person can face even death with confidence and joy. That was the door that God was opening for us: the opportunity to touch lives with the witness to God's power to support us in our daily lives however dire the circumstances.

Because of this, I am nowadays very careful how I pray about things. In the final stages of Roy's illness some dear friends were still praying for his healing. I was perplexed about the right thing to do, so I said, 'Lord, I will pray one more time for this, and after that I will not ask any more.' When I did so, I felt that I had a clear message in my heart from God: 'No, but I am with you; that is all you need' (2 Cor 12:9). Immediately I felt at peace about it, and knew that I need not be concerned any more. I did not want to be praying for something that God did not want for us—I did not want to be outside his will.

Shortly before this a group of us had gathered one evening to pray for Roy, who was then suffering great pain. As we prayed I had an amazing sense of God's timelessness, and felt that he was speaking to me and saying, 'What are days? What are years? Roy will not die before the time I have appointed for him. His life is in my hands. I will have fulfilled my purposes through Roy. Release him to me, set him free because the battle has been won through the prayers of the faithful. There is no guilt and there is no failure, because I am the Lord of time. Rest in the knowledge that the day I choose will be the right day. Don't be afraid—don't you realise that your loss is my gain?' The sense of peace and joy in my heart that evening was immeasurable; we needed to feel no remorse or guilt, only joy and trust that God's will would be done on earth, as it is in heaven.

We all have longings, things we would like to happen if we could have our way. As I write I have three unmarried children, and I often pray that they will find the right partners, and be as blessed and happy in their marriages as their father and I have been. But I have to pull myself up short, and remind myself that I don't know what is best for them. God's best for them may be to remain single. (I am reminded of Sandy Millar, Vicar of Holy Trinity, Brompton, who said gravely, but with a twinkle in his eye: 'I went to theological college, you know, where they taught me how God likes things done!')

Some of our prayers and longings have to be given up when we give our lives to Jesus; we have to let go of our own desires and wills. This is never easy, because it does not come naturally to any of us. We find it hard truly to submit our will to God. At our church we often sing a hymn which includes the line 'Here I am, wholly available'.

I want to be able to sing it, but usually I end up singing, 'Here I am, *fairly* available'—well, there is no point in being less than honest, and God knows me only too well!

I am working at it, though. Deep down I really do want to do what God wants. To be ready for whatever he wants me to do, I feel that I need to live simply, and get rid of all the trappings and encumbrances. I am not a hoarder, and I don't want to keep things for sentimental reasons—they only gather dust! Selwyn Hughes says that there are two ways of being rich: we can be rich 'in the abundance of our possessions' or 'in the fewness of our wants'. For the Christian, I think the second kind of wealth is better. I greatly admired the pope who said, towards the end of his life, 'My bags are packed and I am ready to go.' I should like to feel like that now. Catherine Marshall, a great Christian writer, told about sorting papers after the death of her father.

> Then I picked up Dad's final bank statement. I could scarcely believe what I was seeing. His balance was sixty-five cents.
>
> It is true that you can't take it with you. But whoever heard of someone coming out that even at the end of life?
>
> How typical of Dad! He never did have any money. The salaries of preachers in small towns are notoriously small. Yet always he had been supplied with every need—even to a college education for each of his children and Evergreen Farm for his retirement. His sixty-five-cent statement somehow seemed right.[1]

This seems to me to be the right attitude. Jesus warns us of placing too much faith in worldly possessions in the story of the man who reaped a specially good harvest. He

<hr>

1. Catherine Marshall, *Beyond Our Selves*, Hodder & Stoughton, 1969.

planned to pull down his barns and build bigger ones, and prepare for a wealthy retirement.

> But God said to him, 'You fool! This very night your life will be demanded from you. Then who will get what you have prepared for yourself?' This is how it will be with anyone who stores up things for himself but is not rich towards God (Luke 12:15–21).

I am keen now to get all my affairs in order so that when I die, my children won't have too much to do. When Roy was alive we talked about this, and decided that should we live to a ripe old age, we didn't want to be a nuisance to the children. So while we were still of 'sound mind', we composed a letter to each of them, telling them so. We said that they all had their own lives to live, and they were not to spend time looking after us or visiting us. If necessary they should put us into a nursing home, and not feel guilty about it, because they had in writing what we wanted. Di Parsons joked with us that her children had caused her so much hassle as teenagers that she intended to live as long as possible to get her own back!

My other great longing is to die in harness; to go on being useful to the Lord right to the end, and not to fade away or become a burden to the children. I am grateful that Roy, in spite of the suffering he went through during his illness, nevertheless did not suffer the lingering indignities of old age, or the physical infirmities he would have found it so hard to bear. Rob and Di Parsons often visited us during Roy's illness, and knew him well. Rob says he felt that God concertinaed the final years of Roy's life into two years, giving them a sharp focus and an impact on people which would never have happened if he had died peacefully of old age.

We may never know the truth about God's mysterious ways until this life is over and we see him face to face. Until then, much of what we think and do is a kind of guessing about his purposes. But I believe that only the love of God and the comfort of the Holy Spirit can help us to see that what may appear as a disappointment to us can in fact be a part of God's perfect plan for our lives.

CHAPTER SIX

Living with Grief

For the weakness of my body,
The burdens of each day;
For the nights of doubt and worry,
When sleep has fled away—

The first instinct of grief is very often hibernation. You want to curl up and hide away from others while you struggle to get used to this new state. However, in the first weeks after Roy died I found myself caught up in a whirl of activity. It wasn't just the usual tasks of informing friends and arranging the funeral; there was mail by the sackful and the constant attention of the press. The letters and cards were full of love and consolation, and the requests for interviews were from many journalists who had supported Roy throughout his illness. However, the volume of demands was overwhelming. It was all very tiring.

Grieving is an exhausting process, and I remember that a lot of the time I felt absolutely spent and drained. I was not really surprised by this. I have always been a very active person—my ballet training ensured that I was always very fit and energetic—but I remember that when my mother died, even though it was not unexpected, I seemed to have no energy. I used to get to the top of the stairs with my legs tingling and my muscles weak and floppy, and I would have to lie down on the landing before I could go on, hoping that no one would follow me before I was upright again! Bereavement is always stressful, no matter how well prepared we think we are, or how well we think we are coping. And stress is like an illness; we need to rest and allow the body time to recover.

At the time of Roy's death, Ben had been ill with a tummy bug, and I picked up the same virus almost at once. I felt sick with kidney pains, but I knew that if I told anyone, they would assume that I was suffering from stress. I was, of course, but I knew that wasn't what was causing my illness, because it so closely mirrored Ben's. So I told no one; I didn't want anyone telling me that I was cracking up already! By the time of the funeral I hadn't eaten anything much for three days. I did find that I could drink hot milk with honey in it, and, amazingly, small pieces of a chocolate cake brought as a gift by a friend. So I indulged in that, and found that it settled my tummy. Even now, although I am not usually a great nibbler, I do allow myself to indulge in a little comfort-eating from time to time. When you are grieving you have to be kind to yourself, and not expect too much too soon.

Shortly after Roy's death was announced on the television news, there was a ring at the front door. It was a neighbour—the man who runs the Indian restaurant up the road from us, where Roy and I had often eaten in the past. Roy thought it an excellent restaurant, and often took business people there for lunch, because he loved the curry. The proprietor said how sorry he was to hear of Roy's death.

'It is the custom in our culture,' he said, 'at a time of death, for the neighbours to bring in food for the family. We consider you our neighbour and we would like to cook for you.'

I was very touched by this gesture, and began to say to him, 'It's very kind of you, but please don't bother.' But I was drowned out by the children behind me in the hall, chorusing, 'Oh, yes, please, that would be wonderful!' So for the next two days we had Indian takeaways delivered, which were much appreciated. This kind man is a Muslim, but to show his respect for Roy he attended the funeral in our church. Our hearts were warmed by the dignity and caring of these gifts to us—his presence as well as the food.

Grieving is hard work, for the body as well as for the emotions, and we need to allow for that. It's so easy to drive ourselves from one task to the next, in an effort to keep busy and perhaps not to think too much about things. I found just the opposite. I needed to be able to think, to take stock of the situation and come to terms with the fact of Roy's death. I needed rest, and I had to take care not to let events carry me on so fast that I didn't have time for that. Similarly, it's easy to feel so churned up by our feelings that we don't eat properly; in fact, our bodies need proper food as much as rest to get on with life. These gestures of practical love from our Muslim neighbour helped me to remember this.

Even so, there were times when 'the burdens of each day' threatened to overwhelm me. There were things people used to ask Roy to do—write letters, collect cheques, say a few words to thank fund-raisers—and now they began to ask me to do them. They needed someone to take over Roy's position in the limelight. One day I suddenly realised, 'I'm trying to be Roy *and* me—I'm doing two people's work here!' and after that it became easier to understand, at least, why I was so tired.

For instance, Roy's book, *Now and Then*, was due to be published two weeks after his death. I realised that this made things rather difficult for his publishers, Robson Books, so I said casually, 'If there's anything I can do, just ask'—not thinking for a minute that there would be anything I could do to help them. But in fact it seemed that many people wanted me to give interviews to publicise the book; something that would have been no effort for Roy, but was a new and taxing experience for me.

I often thought, 'If only Roy were here to give me a few tips on what to say, how not to seem nervous in front of the microphone, how to make little jokes to relax people,' but of course if he were, I wouldn't have needed his help! Sometimes it made me feel very lonely.

At one stage, when I was missing Roy dreadfully, I was reading in my Bible study notes about the joy which awaits Christians when we finally see the Lord. 'That's all very well, Jesus,' I said, 'but at this moment I'd rather see Roy!' (Jesus knows our hearts better than we do ourselves, so we have to be real when we're talking to him.) The next day the study notes directed me to Isaiah 54:4–5: 'Remember no more the reproach of your widowhood. For your Maker is your husband—the Lord Almighty is his name—the Holy One of Israel is your Redeemer.' What an answer to my heart's cry! He knew and understood my pain. I remember that when things get on top of me, and I feel lonely and sad. I also have conversations with him: 'OK, Jesus, if Roy were here he'd help me with this . . . if you're my husband you have to help me make decisions!'

There was one day shortly after this when I received out of the blue a most unpleasant and abusive letter which upset me so much that I burst into tears. There was no one to share it with, no one to tell me not to bother about it, and for a while I felt really low. Later that day I had to go to a school prizegiving, and I really needed to be pleasant and cheerful, not moping and sad, so I tried sharing it with the Lord. How should I deal with it? Immediately my thoughts ran on; was I going to let one horrid letter colour my whole weekend? How important was it, anyway, in the light of eternity? Fortunately God gives us a sense of proportion, and I realised that I would be foolish to allow depression even a foothold that day. I decided not to think about it any more. It may seem a small victory over loneliness, but it proved to me that the words in Isaiah could be true for me, and that Jesus could meet my needs, even when I missed my husband's companionship the most.

Once again I realised how important it is not to give way to self-pity. I try on the whole not to rely too much on other people; they have troubles of their own, and though I have many good friends to whom I can go for help with difficulties, I try to keep my troubles to myself. I want to be positive and cheerful when I am with others (and keep my friends!). There's nothing more unattractive than people who are always 'awfulising' everything. I think that I am learning slowly how to get on and cope with life alone—after all, single people who have never married do it all the time. It isn't particularly heroic, only difficult for those of us who have become accustomed to having someone to share our lives.

When Roy died I felt as though I had been cut in two—and in a sense I had. When two people marry, they become 'one flesh', sharing everything. When one partner dies, half of that one flesh is torn away, and the other does indeed feel like only half a person. I am slowly becoming a whole person again. The Lord's healing oil makes the wound heal up more quickly.

Perhaps this is harder for those women whose husbands have regular jobs—or no jobs—whose lives together have involved regular, consistent contact. At least I wasn't used to that. Throughout our marriage we had no routine at all;

sometimes Roy was working from home, at others he would be away for weeks on end. Before I became a Christian I found this very difficult, but afterwards I became more confident and able to cope. Now I am thankful that I had to develop that small degree of independence, because I am to some extent used to being on my own. I am so grateful to God for preparing me in advance.

In fact, it was almost tempting to slip into the old routines I established when Roy was away working. I have had to make myself aware that Roy is never coming back, and force myself to face the pain of that fact. Curiously, this burden of loneliness feels heaviest not at funerals (when I might perhaps expect to feel sad) but at weddings. When a friend's son married soon after Roy died I was greatly moved by the teaching in the service. The minister spoke about relationships, and how they build up over the years, so that an established marriage founded on Christ is a strong building indeed. Our experience was just that, and my sense of loss was intense; I cried all the way through the service—but not at all at a memorial service which I attended later the same day.

Another emotion which can be overwhelming in bereavement is anger. Many people have asked me whether I feel angry with God for 'letting' Roy get cancer. I have to admit that anger has not been one of my emotions. If we trust God, and believe that he has a plan for our lives, then there isn't any point in getting angry with him if things don't work out quite the way we would have liked. We have to submit to his will, and trust that he is working out his purposes for a greater good that we are not yet able to see with our earthbound eyes.

Although I tend not to get angry with God, I am

perfectly capable of feeling very irritated with people—especially those who sometimes make what I consider to be glib, superficially comforting remarks. There were people who said to me, 'Remember, Roy is not far away from you—he's only next door.' I wanted to retort, 'If he were only next door don't you think I'd be there with him?' I refrained, though. I also make a huge effort not to take things too personally, especially when people make insensitive comments. I was chatting to a man once whose wife had gone away for ten days to visit relatives; he complained that he was having trouble sleeping, that he hated being in the bed alone, and generally was immensely miserable. I could easily have become sentimental. Didn't I have a right to be much more miserable than he was? His problem was only going to last for ten days; mine was for ever. I chose not to react and changed the subject!

However, I know many people who suffer from powerful feelings of anger when someone they love suffers or dies, and I'm sure that it is a perfectly normal reaction. It is essential to express it and get it out of our system; it's important to face up to all these strong emotions, deal with them and get rid of them, because if we repress them they only make their way out in physical symptoms of stress, which do our bodies no good.

In the end, the only person hurt by our anger is ourselves (though if we go around snapping at everyone all day there may be some hurt feelings around to deal with!). The best thing to do, as with all such destructive emotions which seem to be beyond our control, is to dump them at the foot of the cross. God can cope with our anger, our hatred, our bitterness and resentment and any other unattractive feelings we are ashamed of. We can't tell him anything he doesn't know already. And he is always waiting for us to admit our weakness, confess the times we have given in to our resentment and fury and taken it out on other people, and tell him we are sorry and ready to start again. Indeed, we cannot start again until we do come to that point of admitting where we have failed. Jim Graham likens this to a foul in a football match: once the foul has been committed and we have recognised it, the referee's whistle has blown. After that it doesn't matter how long we go on playing—there can be no score until the players return to the place where the foul was committed and start again. Similarly, we cannot move forward in our life with God until we go back and confess the sin and accept God's forgiveness.

I recall hearing someone being interviewed on Don Maclean's radio programme, who said, 'Pure joy comes only through the heartbreak of Calvary,' and I believe that this is true. It is the joy of release which enables us to be free and not burdened by our sins; the joy of faith which knows that God is in charge of our world. It bubbles up in spite of all our circumstances because it is an eternal joy which is not transitory nor due to any particular circumstances of our lives.

Once, after I had given a talk about my experiences of marriage and bereavement, a lady came up and told me that since her husband died she had suffered from feelings of anger, bitterness and resentment. I told her that it was all right to experience common human emotions, for we are all human; and that whenever I felt them I placed them at the foot of the cross and gave them over to Jesus. I suggested that when she prayed she should ask Jesus to replace those emotions with the power of the Holy Spirit, and with his love, joy and peace. That night I prayed for her, but I didn't expect to hear from her again. The next day I travelled to Ayr in Scotland, and was surprised to find a fax waiting for me at the office I was going to. It was from my friend from the day before, and said, 'Dear Fiona, it worked! I sat at the feet of Jesus and he bathed me with his peace.'

'The nights of doubt and worry' are another burden of bereavement. When Roy was alive he was the main decision-maker in our family, and I found that the new pressure on me to make decisions alone was stressful. For the first few days I even found making decisions about the funeral difficult, though the family and church were wonderful. They sorted out the flowers in the church, the physical arrangements for the service, and even liaised with Sky TV who were televising the service live, so that I didn't have to worry about anything. The afternoon before the service I went down to the church with my bunch of helium balloons and found the place a hive of activity. The whole congregation had swung into action and everyone was working as a team, relieving me of any anxiety about the organisation.

In the old days Roy had always teased me about being 'a cushion plumper'—meaning someone who goes round last thing at night plumping up the cushions and making sure everything is nice for the next day. When I became a Christian I learned not to worry about being ready for tomorrow. As Roy used to say, 'Get on with your life, but don't forget to smell the roses on the way.' It is a waste of time and energy to worry about the future, because we can't see it or plan for it, and it's pointless to worry about what might never happen. Before I became a Christian I used to worry about everything; now I just pray about everything and trust in God to help me. I try to practise a verse from Philippians: 'Don't worry about anything; instead, pray about everything; tell God your needs and don't forget to thank him for his answers. If you do this you will experience God's peace, which is far more wonderful than the human mind can understand' (Philippians 4:6–7, Living Bible). Curiously, when we had real trouble in our lives, I believe that God prepared me for it, so that when Roy's second bout of cancer began, I was not surprised—just disappointed. We had already learned to trust God one day at a time, and not to look further.

Nowadays worries seldom rob me of sleep; I'm usually too tired to do anything but collapse thankfully into bed! But in the weeks before Roy died I slept very little, because I was nursing him alone at home, and he was often restless and in pain at night. I got used to snatching naps when he did, day or night, and for the last week I didn't undress at night but lay on top of the bed in a tracksuit, ready to get up if he needed me.

Some of those nights were very dark indeed. There were moments when I asked, 'Where is God in all this?'—times when he didn't seem to be answering our prayers or taking away Roy's suffering. That was when I felt most alone, as though I was in a dark tunnel and there was no way out but to keep plodding forward without hope or help or light. Three months afterwards I spent a quiet day's retreat at Highmoor Hall, and came across this piece by Ulrich Shaeffer, which perfectly reflected my feelings at this time.

My outstretched hands are becoming accustomed
to the solitude into which you have thrown me
more alone
than I could ever bear to be

I am learning to live
with the death you have chosen for me
more painful than any death
I have ever chosen to go through

My eyes are adapting
to the darkness you have chosen for me
darker than any darkness
I ever knew or chose

I am learning to recognise
the many disguises of your love
deeper than any love
I have ever experienced

And slowly it dawns on me
Being lonely is: turning to you
death is: a deep and joyous life
darkness is: finally seeing your light
and love is: being born over and over again.[1]

Again, back in the days before I was a Christian I was always a prey to worries and fears, and when Roy was away (which was often) I was frequently unable to sleep. After I became a Christian I learned the secret of not worrying, but trusting in God and resting in him. 'I will lay down in peace and sleep, for though I am alone, O Lord, you will keep me safe' (Psalm 4:8, Living Bible). I would pray each night, 'Lord, please will you wrap me in your loving arms,' and then I would find it easy to fall asleep.

Generally, my feeling about sleeplessness, from the days when I did suffer from it, is that the best thing is to get up and do something, and not let it worry you. If you aren't

---

1. Ulrich Schaeffer, *Into Your Light*, InterVarsity Press.

asleep you probably don't need to be, and lying awake worrying about it doesn't help. Insomnia is nearly always linked to stress and being unable to relax; a hot drink, a good book and being resigned to being awake often does the trick!

My favourite story about insomnia was told by Clive Calver at yet another Spring Harvest. It was during the Blitz in London: night after night people would go down into the air raid shelters, and what with the fear and worry and the distant noises of bombs and sirens, few would be able to get much sleep. One little old lady, however, was always able to settle down and sleep peacefully. When someone asked her how she did it, she replied, 'I used to find it hard to sleep down here. So I prayed about it, and God said to me, "I'm awake all night anyway; there's no point in both of us being up!"'

No matter what the burdens we have to carry each day, or what worries beset us at night, we have the comfort of knowing that Jesus is there beside us to take all our cares upon himself and release us into confidence, joy and peace. For all these things, we have Jesus—what a wonderful friend.

CHAPTER SEVEN

Facing the Future

Needing reassurance,
And the will to start again;
A steely-eyed endurance,
The strength to fight and win—

People say that there is a process to grief; that your feelings and responses change as time passes, and that eventually, although the pain of bereavement never goes away, you get used to bearing it. I think that is probably true, but as I look back over the time since Roy died, I am surprised to see how little my attitude has changed. Of course the sharpest pain of loss has become a little less intense, but my feelings about his death have not altered.

On the morning after Roy's death I was interviewed by the Revd Steve Williams for the BBC Radio Merseyside 'Daybreak' programme. Listening to it again recently, I was struck by the fact that everything I said then is still true today, and that I would make the same responses now as I did then. Part of it went like this:

Fiona, you're in the hearts and minds of everyone on Merseyside this morning.

I'm very aware of that . . . I feel as though I'm being carried along on a life-raft at the moment. It's wonderful.

How are you feeling now?

I'm fine, actually . . . the relief of knowing that Roy isn't in pain any longer is so great . . . I've got peace because I know he's at peace.

Knowing that this moment was coming, how did you and Roy prepare for it?

We've had two and a half years to prepare for the fact that Roy might die, so we've had a long time to talk things through . . . in fits and starts, of course, because he did get better at one time. In the last three months we've known that it was coming to an end, and we've talked about life. We're just so grateful that we've had a really good relationship. One of the things we realised early on was the strength of a good relationship, because the only emotion we would experience was sadness that it was coming to an end. If people have relationships that are wrong, that they haven't been able to put right, there can be remorse, and guilt and so on . . . we're glad we didn't have any of those to cope with, so that made it a lot easier. And because we're Christians we have hope of eternal life and that assurance, and great excitement about what was to come. I think Roy sensed the excitement of what was ahead of him; there was no fear of death because of his faith.

How have you sensed that?

He had a few glimpses of heaven before he died . . . one day he kept seeing beautiful lights and telling me how beautiful they were . . . it lasted a few minutes and then went away. . . I think these little glimpses just assured him of what was to come.

Was there any one single piece of advice Roy gave to you, when you faced this together?

We talked about all of life . . . I know he would be really fed up with me if I didn't pull myself together and get on with life! He was thrilled, several years ago, when once the children had flown the nest and were really independent, that I had a burning interest of my own to keep me going. I didn't suffer from the empty nest syndrome of wondering what to do with my life, because that was already rolling. I had the opportunity to share my faith with people—I'd been invited on lots of occasions to go to meetings and share what my faith means to me. It's a real privilege, and he knew that was going to continue. As Christians we live our lives for God, because we have always asked the Lord to guide us for the next step. We only want to do what God wants us to do—in a simple and basic way, nothing dramatic. That encouraged him, because he knew that I wouldn't just sit on my backside and mope!

That seems to be a remarkable approach so soon after the event. Many people would be interested to hear how you can speak in this way.

Well, I'm very normal, very ordinary—we've cried a lot, but we've also laughed a lot over the last two years. We've never taken things too seriously in our family—some things are serious of course, but we can never stay serious for long, and there's been a tremendous amount of laughter in the house yesterday and today. We do have a happy, bright and positive outlook on life. I think that helps.

How has your Christian faith affected how you've approached this?

Oh, it's been everything. It has strengthened such a lot since we've gone through this. I heard someone preaching some-where once, and he said that problems are growth activators, and I latched onto that because it's true. You do grow through the difficult times. You sail along through the easy times, but you have to grow, otherwise you crumble in the difficult times. We've learned so much through the problems that we've both said, all the way through, that we wouldn't be without the experience. It's been brilliant. My Christian faith has strengthened. I know with a deep conviction and assurance that God is in control of every part of our lives.

You felt that at the actual moment when Roy died?

Yes—there wasn't anything dramatic. He just gradually got weaker and slipped away. But I knew where he'd gone; I had a deep assurance that he was with the Lord and I didn't have to be anxious at all for him. There was a sense of real relief because he suffered a lot and that was hardest for me—all that had gone, and it was lifted from him and from me. So in a sense there was rejoicing—I felt that the angels were really rejoicing in heaven about it all.

. . . What do you imagine your emotions will be when the foundation stone is laid, after all Roy's campaigning for the Cause for Hope Appeal?

I don't know—it will be very tough, won't it? But I'll be very proud, because I think Roy will be very proud at that moment. He said one day that there'll be a little sunbeam shining down on it—so we shall watch for that sunbeam.

How would you want Roy to be remembered?

With joy, with happiness and fun, and that he's done something worthwhile with his life.

None of my feelings about Roy's death have changed since then. I have been through times of great sadness and of course I still miss him and always will, but my basic trust in God has remained the same. Lots of people have made gloomy predictions that I wasn't sufficiently depressed and that there would come a time of reckoning when I would 'crack up' under the strain. I'm sorry to disappoint them, but I haven't shown any signs of it yet.

On the first anniversary of Roy's death I received many cards remembering him, and I was very moved that so many people took the time to think of me. Jim Graham, our pastor, and his wife Anne sent me some flowers with the simple message, 'With deep gratitude for precious memories of the past and certain glorious hope for the future,' and that made me cry, because they remembered him and the memories were precious to them too. 'Hope for the future' was exactly right as well because part of the challenge of bereavement is the need to face the future alone with hope; 'the will to start again'.

Roy had defined my role for me at the start of our marriage. 'You look after the home and take care of the family. I'll take care of my career. I don't even want you to talk to my agent. That's my business.' He had seen many a marital conflict caused by wives interfering with show business career moves, and he was determined that it wasn't going to happen to us! This didn't mean we never discussed his plans together, and he would often ask my advice, but the final decision was his. I was therefore quite content to be what he wanted me to be and happy to stay in the background.

So it was quite a shock, in the April after Roy died, when I was asked to do an interview with Gloria Hunniford at Pebble Mill. I was extraordinarily nervous about this for several reasons: Roy had always done the interviews before, and I still felt that I was much too shy to interview well; I felt exposed and vulnerable doing things alone, because I wasn't used to being in hotels without him (even going down to breakfast alone was a challenge); and we had spent months in Birmingham during the last months of his life, when he was in *Pickwick*, and I felt that everywhere would hold painful memories for me. Nevertheless I was determined to rise to the challenge of doing things and facing people without him, so I went. I did the interview, and I also made myself go round the Birmingham stores where I had shopped with Roy, and recalled the conversations we had and the jokes we laughed over together. It was my way of facing up to what I was afraid of, and proving that I could do it.

I continue to be very busy. I seem to be constantly

dashing around the country on behalf of the Cause for Hope Foundation, which is wonderful because the fund-raising is still going well—I know Roy would be delighted! It is strange because I know I am being asked as a sort of substitute for Roy, who became a symbol for the people the appeal is designed to help. Recently I received a cheque from a Manchester lunch club, where an entertainment was given by the cast of *Pickwick*, and Bernie Clifton performed a sketch which used to be done by Roy and Jimmy James, so it was very much like old times.

I find all this activity therapeutic, because it means I have no time to sit around and mope. I take the time to think about Roy, and I have not tried to escape in any way from the reality of bereavement. However, I don't want to spend the rest of my life dwelling on thoughts of death and widowhood. Sometimes I do feel a pang of guilt that I don't seem to be 'mourning' in the traditional sense, but with a lively young family and a busy church life, I would make everyone's lives miserable if I insisted on sitting at home and doing nothing but grieving.

At home I keep a picture of Roy on the landing half-way up the stairs, and as I pass it on my way upstairs I always stop, kiss my fingers and touch them to Roy's face—it's a little gesture that's important to me. But sometimes I'm in such a hurry that I gallop upstairs two at a time and call out, 'Sorry, can't stop—too busy!' I know Roy would enjoy that—it's his fault I'm so busy in the first place! He loved to quote the catch-phrase of Oliver Hardy: 'Another fine mess you've gotten me into!'

One regret is that nowadays I have less time to see friends than when I was a full-time wife and mother and at home all day. But I try to make dates in my diary and ensure that I don't lose touch. I also get quite tired with all the travelling and speaking, but I am amazed that when I am doing what God wants, I always seem to have enough energy to go round. I may go to bed absolutely exhausted, but I always wake with a spring in my heel and my energy renewed. 'Those who hope in the Lord will renew their strength. They will soar on wings like eagles; they will run and not grow weary, they will walk and not be faint' (Isaiah 40:31).

All this is part of having 'the will to start again'—being willing to look for what God wants us to do, and then going for it, however weak we may think we are. Our ability or lack of it is of little account when God is in charge—he enables us to do his will; the crucial part for us is getting on with it!

Before I became a Christian I knew a lot about what the Bible says, but had no more thought of putting it into action than of speaking in Hebrew. It never occurred to me that the Bible could be relevant to my everyday life; I thought it was an informative story about what happened a long time ago, a long way away. Now I realise that the Bible is God's word for us, and it tells us how to live and how to follow Jesus in our daily life, but it isn't any help to us unless we are prepared to act on its instructions.

I liken it to studying a Rosemary Conley fitness plan: we can read about keeping fit, look at the sets of exercises to improve our muscles, and check out the diet sheets and recipes. We can see what an excellent system the whole thing is—but we won't get any fitter unless we actually do the exercises, throw away the cream buns and keep to the plan. In the same way we can read God's word every day, but it's no good just agreeing with it; unless we are prepared to put it into practice we won't change our lives and we won't realise that it works.

There may be many bad times when we are 'needing reassurance'. Then, the Bible tells us, 'Be joyful always; pray continually; give thanks in all circumstances, for this is God's will for you in Christ Jesus' (1 Thessalonians 5: 16–18). It may be hard for us to give thanks *for* the bad times, but we can at least give thanks *in* the bad times, and often when we make that effort we find that our attitude is transformed. Simply putting God back into the heart of our circumstances is often enough to restore our sense of proportion and enable us to see a way through. I know that if I praise God when things are bad, I am often lifted out of my dark mood and given the grace to see things with God's eternal perspective— it's amazing how small some of our concerns can seem then. It also reassures me, by restoring my faith in his overall plan for my life. I find it exciting that his plan for me is still unfolding, and I marvel at what he does, and at the unique opportunities which emerge when we let God have his way.

For instance, I still have two or three speaking engage- ments each week for Christian groups; I may be present- ing the Christian message to people who have scarcely heard it, or supporting and encouraging Christians who are faithfully trying to walk in God's way. Sometimes people come and pour out their personal sorrows, and all I can do is listen to them, and give them my time and attention, and show the love of Jesus for them in that way. Through this work I meet people I would never otherwise have met or been involved with, and I thank God for the opportunities he gives me.

I am always amazed by the way God trains and pre- pares us for things, long before we have any thought of doing them. Before Roy died I had never done any work on television, but I had sat in with Roy and I had seen how TV studios work. I still feel nervous and inadequate, but I get on with it, as Roy used to. (He much preferred live entertainment because of the immediate contact and rapport with people it gave him.)

As time goes on I have become more confident about speaking. The most nerve-wracking thing I ever did was speaking at a Billy Graham meeting at Mission '84. I had been involved in some of the preparation work—attending regional coffee mornings to build up interest—and then I was asked to speak at the main meetings at Anfield and Ipswich. Anfield was packed and the organisation was tremendous. There was a choir of two hundred on the dais behind us! We rehearsed thoroughly, working out how we would get to our seats and in what order we would speak, but nothing could have prepared me for the sight of that stadium. We were so far away from the crowd that the people looked like ants in the distance; I couldn't see their faces at all, and I was sure that I would not be able to speak normally.

Fortunately, just before the big day I had asked a lovely old lady at church if she would pray for me, and she said, 'My dear, just imagine you're talking to one woman in her sitting room.' It was the best advice I could have had, and I followed it, and got through my task somehow.

I'm not always a success. I once spoke at a meeting, and at the end the vicar got up and said, 'Thank you for coming, but I disagree with everything you've said,' which made me feel rather bad. Such criticism hurts, but if we believe we are doing God's work, then we have to have that 'steely-eyed endurance' to go on with the task God has set us to do. Of course, if we disregard criticism, we must also treat praise in the same way, and not take it personally. We must accept praise and pass it straight on to God, to whom it belongs. We are only the channel for his message. Len Moules said that we should pray for our preachers when they go up into the pulpit but we must also pray for them when they come down. In other words, we must pray that they will deliver God's message well, and also pray that whether they succeed or fail they will not take it too much to heart. After all, no one succeeds every time, and I try to learn by my mistakes.

My favourite audience is one consisting of young mothers, because then I am usually speaking from my own experience of bringing up a family of four. I love to see the recognition in their faces when they realise that they are not the only ones with certain feelings, or who behave in a certain way. I cheerfully recount some of my worst mistakes, and enjoy their laughter, and seeing the little whispered conversations springing up as they share in my experiences. I have a real heart for young mothers and want to encourage them; so often their work goes unnoticed and unappreciated and their self-esteem is low. I think it is important to build up their sense of self-worth, for in bringing up the next generation they are engaged in the most important work of all. They need to be affirmed in their role of homemaker and mother, something society doesn't do these days, making them feel like second-class citizens if they are not earning money outside the home.

My enjoyment of this work is part of the general joy I have in living. When I became a Christian God gave me the gift of peace, and freed me from my fears: 'I am leaving you with a gift—peace of mind and heart. And the peace I give isn't fragile like the peace the world gives. So don't be troubled or afraid' (John 14:27, Living Bible). I did not realise it at first, but when Roy died, God added the gift of joy: 'I have told you this so that you will be filled with my joy. Yes, your cup of joy will overflow' (John 15:11, Living Bible). You can't manufacture joy, or pretend it; it's either there or it's not. It was only when I looked back after the first six months that I realised that even though I had been grieving, the joy was still bubbling up in me. Jesus wants our cup of joy to be full—so it's our fault if it's usually half empty!

D.L. Moody says,

> There is a difference between happiness and joy. Happiness is caused by things which happen around me, and circumstances will mar it, but joy flows right on through trouble; joy flows on through the dark; joy flows in the night as well as in the day; joy flows all through persecution and opposition; it is an unceasing fountain bubbling up in the heart; a secret spring which the world cannot see and doesn't know anything about. The Lord gives his people perpetual joy when they walk in obedience to him.

It's the power of the Holy Spirit which fills us with joy, and it's the same power which gives us that 'steely-eyed endurance' and 'the will to fight and win'. Before I became a Christian I often suffered with depression, which clouded my days and spoiled our family life. Roy used to say that I had a 'death-wish'—not really to die, but to kill off any joy and happiness in my life. After Roy died, there were moments when I longed to die as well; not out of any gloomy death-wish but just to be with him and be with the Lord. I wanted to take the easy way out of what I knew was going to be the uphill struggle of bereavement, and all the battles I was going to have to fight against loneliness and self-pity. Part of me was willing to work for the Lord for as long as he wanted to keep me on this earth—but oh, how much easier to go to heaven and miss out the struggle! That was when I was reminded of something Roy used to say to me when I was depressed and worn down by all the jobs I had to do: 'You will insist on thinking about everything you've got to do all at once, instead of thinking about one thing at a time!'

So I disciplined myself to take one day at a time, and trust God for the rest: 'Therefore do not worry about tomorrow, for tomorrow will worry about itself' (Matthew 6:34)—another example of putting God's word into action in our lives. Once I held on to that verse and practised it, I found that the difficulties I had built up in my mind melted away and joy took over.

That is why I don't worry when people say that I shouldn't be cheerful, or that because I am, I can't have come to terms with Roy's death and the fact of my widowhood. I have faced the darkest times of my life and I have proved that 'for this I have Jesus'. I know that he will uphold and support me even through the worst problems life can offer. I feel like the man in the 'Footprints' poem, who saw two sets of footprints in the sand, one belonging to him and the other to God. He complained that at the lowest and saddest times of his life there was only one set of footprints, and said, 'I don't understand why in times when I needed you most, you would leave me.' And God replied, 'I love you and I would never leave you during your times of trials and suffering. When you see only one set of footprints, it was then that I carried you.'

I certainly have had the sense of being 'carried' by God, sometimes through the prayers and love of other Christians, through the dark times of the last few years. I have discovered for myself the truth of Psalm 23:

> Even though I walk
> through the valley of the shadow of death
> I will fear no evil
> for you are with me.

When we begin to understand this, we learn to rely on God, our only hope, the only one who is reliable and trustworthy, the only one to whom we can turn for security and comfort. It is our daily walk with Jesus which enables us to discover the riches of God's love:

> You prepare a table before me
> in the presence of my enemies.
> You anoint my head with oil;
> my cup overflows.
> Surely goodness and mercy will follow me
> all the days of my life,
> and I will dwell in the house of the Lord
> for ever (Psalm 23:5–6).

A widower wrote: 'For months I never imagined that life would be good to me again, or that I would want it to be good. But it is, and I do. My grief has been far the deepest, most significant thing that has ever happened to me.' This strikes a chord with my experience. As I said in the interview I gave the day after Roy died: 'Problems are growth activators.' When we face devastating circumstances we re-evaluate all our ideas about life and death, and for some, this is the first step on the way to discovering what is truly important to them in life. When we see the reality of God's power working in our lives our faith grows fast. We can never fully understand God's purposes, but sometimes when we look back we can see results—extraordinary, unimaginable results which we would never have predicted or chosen for ourselves—

and we can only wonder at God's grace which can bring such fruits of love, joy and peace out of pain.

Roy's path to death led through cancer, which caused him terrible suffering. It was not the path he would have chosen, but he accepted it and said, late in his illness, 'I wouldn't have been without this experience.' We both learned such a lot about the everlasting arms of God, always beneath us and supporting us, that no price was too high to pay for that assurance. Shortly before he died, a friend told us that when praying she saw Roy 'in the palm of God's hand', and that was what it felt like—love surrounding us and holding us up.

Roy took that path all the way to the doors of death, and passed through into God's garden and the bright light of eternal life that he had glimpsed in the last few days of his illness. I walked beside him for a while, but my path has turned aside now because the Lord has other things still for me to do.

It has been hard to learn to journey on without the love and support of my husband beside me, but I am becoming braver and more accustomed to my situation as time passes. Margaret Torrie founded Cruse, the National Organisation for the Widowed, in 1959. In her book *Begin Again* she says, 'The remarkable discovery we can make is that love has not deserted us, and that it is available now in a new way. Our own willingness to love and to give in the world about us is the secret of recovery and the new beginning.'[1] In many ways the end of this book is part of a new beginning for me.

In January 1996 I flew out alone to visit my daughter Julia who is working in Peru. The journey was made

1. Margaret Torrie, *Begin Again*, Dent, 1970.

unnecessarily complicated by a series of delays and barely made connections, which resulted in me arriving in Lima on time, while Julia was expecting me to be several hours late. Waiting alone in a deserted airport, in a country where I could not speak the language, on a day when I had already been up for twenty-six hours, was a fairly shattering experience. At that moment I felt as alone as I have ever felt. If Roy had been with me we would have joked and laughed and the whole thing would have been fun. As it was, I discovered the kindness of strangers, in the shape of some friendly and protective waiters who showed me where to store my luggage and allowed me to sit in their restaurant over a cup of coffee for several hours.

I eventually met up with Julia and we got back to her flat just in time for her to leave for work, while I showered, unpacked and went to bed.

These daunting experiences paled into insignificance once I started to appreciate Julia's life and to travel around with her. Sometimes she teaches English to businessmen in Lima, and at others she teaches jewellery-making to people in the shanty towns. Because of a complex political situation and terrorism in the countryside, many people have been forced out of their mountain villages, where they had farmed the land for generations, and into the cities where there is no work for them. Julia hit on the idea of making jewellery because the materials are cheap to obtain, and it is a skill which the people seem able to pick up easily. In fact, they show great excitement and a sense of achievement when they realise that at last they have the possible means of making a living. The ability to be self-sufficient restores their dignity and they always greeted Julia with great enthusiasm.

One day Julia took me to a village near Chosica, about two hours' drive north of Lima, which we reached by means of three different *combis* (anything from a minibus to a broken-down dormobile van, usually in various states of decay) and finally a *collectivo* (an elderly Chevrolet with eight seats squashed into the back). Driving in Peru is an adventure in itself, as most of the vehicles would never be allowed on the road in England, and driving standards are quite different. As a journalist said, 'They generally drive on the right—unless they feel like driving on the left. It is considered courteous to slow down at red traffic lights!'

The shanty town was a revelation to me. These pathetic, half-built houses were home to thousands of people, perched on the sides of the mountains. The mountains themselves are ugly, rising out of the desert which stretches for hundreds of miles along the coast. There is no rainfall to settle the dust, so the sandstone rocks and scant vegetation are all covered in it. The Quechua Evangelical Church consisted of half-built brick walls, covered by a bit of corrugated-iron roofing. At the back was a separate area with a single butane gas ring for cooking; in front was a little pulpit with some flowers on it, some benches and a table around which a dozen young women were waiting for Julia.

We were welcomed with incredible warmth, and while some of them carried on with their jewellery-making, the older women prepared a simple but delicious meal on their one burner. It was ground fresh corn from the cob, mixed with milk and eggs and either a tiny piece of cheese or some sugar and raisins. This was spread by the spoon-ful onto the leaves of the corn, which were folded and placed in an enormous pan of boiling water. We realised that we were being invited to a banquet, prepared with more love and sacrifice than if we had been going to a palace.

The pastor told us about their struggles and their needs, sent greetings to our church in England from the Quechua church, and asked us to pray for them. It was clear that they needed money, but they did not ask for that, only our prayers and fellowship. They are lovely, happy, Christian people, and somehow I came away from them feeling happy. In spite of their poverty they did not suffer from the squalor and hopelessness I had seen elsewhere in Lima; I was amazed at the fastidiousness with which they kept everything spotless in such primitive conditions. Everywhere there were lines of washing flapping in the breeze, and the children's clothes were clean, and their shining black hair neatly groomed. The thought of surviving one night on the side of that dusty mountain in the heat appalled me, yet their love and appreciation of Julia's help made it hard to leave.

When I travelled to Peru I knew that I would be brought face to face with life in the raw, in such poverty-stricken surroundings. I knew that Julia faced it daily and that she had a special love for these people, but I am ashamed to admit that I hadn't wanted to be confronted by what I knew existed there. Would it make me feel guilty and uncomfortable about my own life at home? I knew many people who said that having once visited a Third-World country their lives were never the same again.

I don't think my life will ever be the same again, but not for the reasons I was expecting. It was an enriching experience as well as a heart-breaking one. I will have a new zest to support and pray for those people, and a new awareness of the relative unimportance of material possessions. These people had nothing, but they were rich and happy because they had Jesus.

As I went to bed that night I said to Julia, 'That could have been us, if we had been born here. We have no power to choose where we're born or into what circumstances, but we can choose what we do with them. These people have chosen Jesus' way, and their smiles tell it all: "For this we have Jesus."'

I have described these experiences because they made a startling impact on me in many ways. First, because I enjoyed the adventure of travelling alone. I missed Roy's company but I was excited by the new experiences and by the sense of achievement I gained from getting myself alone across the world and back in one piece! Secondly, I gained a new admiration for my daughter, who is making so much of her life, and working as a channel for God's love to reach and help people.

Thirdly, I have gained a new perspective on giving. We all see television films of Third-World countries; we know all about conditions and economics and climate and lots of other facts. I knew about these things with my head, but now I know them with my heart. Before I left one old lady came up to me ('*La Mama de la hermana Hulya*'—Julia's mother), took a little paste brooch in the shape of a tortoise which she was wearing, and pinned it to my shirt. 'Forgive us for the way we are,' she said, 'but we want you to know that we love you and we are very happy.' Their love and happiness touched my heart, and inspired me to love and care for them as Julia does.

It has shown me that for as long as we live, God may have new beginnings for us, new experiences and new lessons of his love that he wants us to learn. Our path may be through 'green pastures' or through the valley of the shadow of death, but it is always the same Good Shepherd who leads us, and Jesus is with us at every stage in our journey.

> Because the heart of our God is full of mercy towards us, the Light of Heaven shall come to visit us—to shine on those who lie in darkness and under the shadow of death, and to guide our feet into the path of peace (Luke 1:68).

The first Sunday after it was confirmed that Roy had cancer, the pastor was preaching and repeated the words 'All is well, all shall be well' several times. They stood out for me and I treasured them. When the cancer returned the second time I received a card from Sister Ursula, a friend and former teacher of Julia's, which had almost the same words on it: 'All shall be well and all shall be well . . . thou shalt see it thyself that all manner of things shall be well'—words from the Thirteenth Revelation of the Lady Julian of Norwich, who wrote her *Revelations of Divine Love* in the fourteenth century after a period of great pain and sickness. The simple faith she expressed touched my heart, and I can still speak those words with assurance.

Roy was as solid as a rock throughout our marriage, and he was always a rock to support me. But if I had built my life on my marriage alone, I would have fallen apart when he died. Instead my life is built on the solid rock of Jesus Christ, and that fact is my strength to continue as long as God chooses to keep me on this earth. I am content to accept whatever he wants for my life. So as I face tomorrow, and the next day, I place my trust in Jesus to lead me on. Whatever happens, 'for this I have Jesus'.

Make a note of these other titles from the Castle family—

Give Us This Day

This was Fiona Castle's first book, telling of her own youth, her marriage to Roy and their life together. She tells of her coming to faith, and of the way in which that faith sustained them both through the early days of Roy's illness.

ISBN 0 85476 414 3

Also available read on cassette by Fiona – KPC008

Ben and Roy's Big Celebration

In the months before his death, Roy Castle got together with his son Ben to record this album. It celebrates life and their shared love of music, particularly jazz, and includes such tracks as 'I am a new creation' and 'Jesus, we celebrate your victory'.

Cassette KMC735   CD KMCD735

Breathe Easy

Ben Castle is an accomplished musician, playing saxophone, flute and clarinet. He gathered together some of the most gifted big band and jazz musicians in the UK to record his arrangements of well-known hymns and worship songs, along with some of his own compositions. The album is dedicated to Roy's memory.

Cassette KMC866   CD KMCD866

Books and music are available from your local Christian bookshop or, in case of difficulty, from Kingsway Publications, Lottbridge Drove, Eastbourne, East Sussex BN23 6NT (Tel: 0800 378446).

Other titles from Kingsway Publications—

No Greater Love by Joy Bath with Shirley Collins

Joy Bath was a missionary midwife. She caught AIDS and paid the highest price in her service for others. Her story is moving and inspiring.
ISBN 0 85476 578 6

What Happens When We Die? by Dr Alison Morgan

Many have sought the answer to this question, calling on evidence from near-death experiences, or even supernatural revelation. What do they say? What are we to believe? Alison Morgan decided to 'shop around' to see if a clear picture could be formed by a careful examination of the claims made by various religions, the testimonies of those who say they have 'been there', and scientific research. Her conclusions are remarkably unqualified and clear, and offer a challenge and a hope few will want to ignore.
ISBN 0 85476 336 8

Bereaved by Ian Knox

There comes a time in all our lives when we lose someone, or something, dear to us. But while personal loss may be inevitable, our feelings will not be so predictable. Ian Knox looks at many different kinds of bereavement and offers an invaluable aid for the bereaved, and for those offering comfort and support.
ISBN 0 85476 379 1

All titles are available from your local Christian bookshop or, in case of difficulty, from Kingsway Publications, Lottbridge Drove, Eastbourne, East Sussex BN23 6NT (Tel: 0800 378446).